LITERARY SOMERSET

LITERARY
SOMERSET

JAMES CROWDEN

First Published in 2010 by
Flagon Press
Forge House, Fore Street
Winsham, Chard
Somerset TA20 4DY

www.james-crowden.co.uk

ISBN 978-0-9562778-0-0

British Library and Cataloguing-in-Production Data.
A catalogue record for this book is available from
The British Library.

Design by Andrew Crane
Typeset in Bitstream Carmina
Printed and bound by Butler Tanner & Dennis
Frome, Somerset

THE COUNTY OF *SOMERSET*, commonly call'd *Somersetshire*, is a large and plentiful County. On the north the Severn-Sea bears upon it, on the west it bounds upon Devonshire, on the south upon Dorsetshire, upon the east upon Wiltshire and part of Gloucestershire. The soil is very rich, especially for grain and pasturage, tis very populous and tolerably well furnished with havens. Some think that this name was first given it because the air is gentle, and as it were a *Summer air* in those parts... in which sense the Britains at this day call it *Glad arhaf* translating the word out of our language.

But the truth is, as in summer time, it may really be called a *Summer-country*, so no less in the winter season be called a *winter-country*: so wet, moist and marshy it is for the most part; which creates a great deal of trouble to travellers. However I shall not scruple to believe that this name was certainly given it from *Somerton*, formerly the chief town of the County, since *Asser*, a very ancient author, calls it everywhere, the county of *Somertun*.

WILLIAM CAMDEN 1584

CONTENTS

PART TWO
FROM NETHER STOWEY
TO COMBE FLOREY

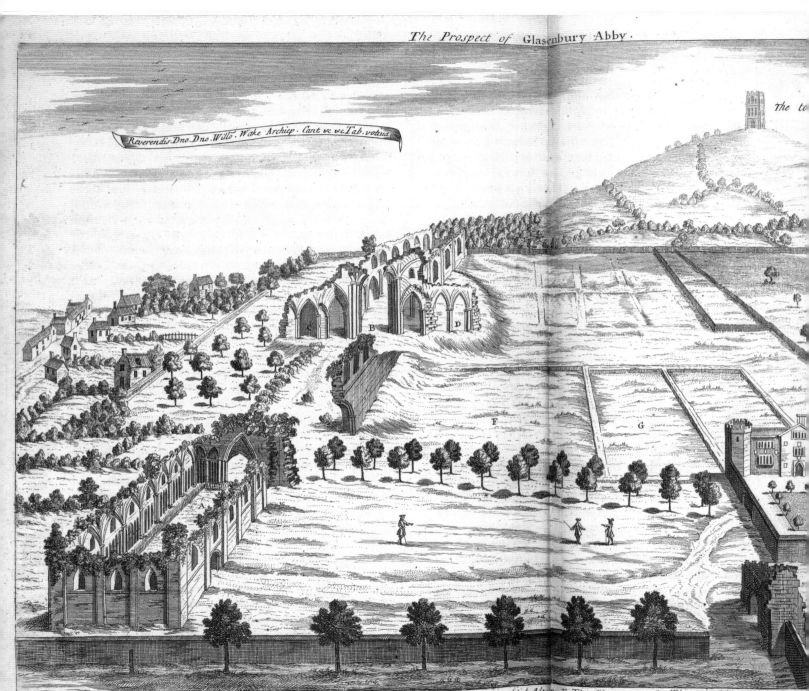

Reverendis. Dno. Dno. Willo. Wake Archiep. Cant &c &c Tab. votiua.

A. St. Josephs chappel B. The Abby Church. C. St. Marys chappel D. Edgars chappel. E. The high Alter. F. The Cloysters. G. The Hall. H. The Abbots

37

I. The Abbots Lodging.   Stukeley del,

PART ONE

FROM BATH TO EAST COKER

Ruins of
Glastonbury Abbey
by William Stukeley
1724

1 FROM THE RUIN TO THE WIFE OF BATH

GEOGRAPHICALLY Somerset was a key part of the Anglo-Saxon kingdom of Wessex and it is no coincidence that some of the earliest literature in the English language should be associated with the county. With the Danes on the doorstep, it was a rough time when language and politics were being hammered out line by line. Poetry concentrated on tales of noble deeds and the fighting spirit, devotion and banishment, mystery, death and loneliness. The same language also kept historical chronicles and marked significant events.

We still marvel at the strength and elegance of the Anglo-Saxon poetry and can only wonder at the literary gems that might have been lost.

Author of The Ruin – c.8th century AD

POET / Visited Bath with parchment in hand

The identity of this brilliant wordsmith, the anonymous wandering poet, still remains a mystery today. *The Ruin* is believed to be the earliest poem in the English language and describes the poet's feelings and impressions of wandering round the ruined city of Bath three centuries after the Romans left. The original copy survives in the Exeter Book on two leaves of badly scarred parchment charred around the edges. The fine-wrought description of the overgrown ruins can only be of *Aquae Sulis*, an important Roman city that we now know simply as Bath. The poem is incomplete. It is, however, a very powerful piece of writing and a fine example of the English language that was once spoken in Somerset, the land of the *Sumorsetae* or the summer settlers. The best translation from the Anglo-Saxon is by Michael Alexander of Stirling University who now lives in Wells.

The poem includes such wonderful composite words as *gravesgrasp, earthgrip, horngabled, mood-glad, goldbright* and *broad-dominion* words which inspired poets such as Gerard Manley Hopkins and writers such as J.R.R. Tolkien who was himself an expert on Anglo-Saxon.

THE RUIN

Well-wrought this wall: Wierds broke it.
The stronghold burst....

Snapped rooftrees, towers fallen,
the work of Giants, the stonesmiths,
mouldereth.
       Rime scoureth gate towers
       Rime on mortar.

Shattered the showershields, roofs ruined
age under-ate them.
       And the wielders and wrights?
Earthgrip holds them- gone, long gone,
fast in gravesgrasp while fifty fathers
and sons have passed.

       Wall stood,
grey lichen, red stone, kings fell often,
stood under storms, high arch crashed-
stands yet the wallstone, hacked by weapons,
by files grim ground...
...shone the old skilled work
...sank to loam crust.

Mood quickened mind, and a man of wit,
cunning in rings, bound bravely the wall base
with iron, a wonder.

Bright were the buildings, halls where springs ran
high horngabled, much throng noise;
these many meadhalls men filled
with loud cheerfulness: Wierd changed that.

Came days of pestilence, on all sides men fell dead,
death fetched off the flower of people;
where they stood to fight, waste places
and on the acropolis, ruins.

       Hosts who would build again
shrank to the earth. Therefore are these courts dreary
and that red arch twisteth tiles,
wryeth from roof ridge, reacheth groundwards...
Broken blocks...

       There once many a man
mood-glad, goldbright, of gleams garnished
flushed with wine-pride, flashing war-gear,
gazed on wrought gemstones, on gold, on silver,
on wealth held and hoarded, on light-filled amber,
on this bright burg of broad dominion.

Stood stone house; wide streams welled
hot from source, and a wall all caught
in its bright bosom that the baths were
hot at hall's hearth; that was fitting...

Thence hot streams loosed ran over hoar stone
unto the ring tank...
    ...It is a kingly thing
    ...city...

Translated by MICHAEL ALEXANDER

Saint Aldhelm c.639–709

BISHOP, POET AND SCHOLAR / Died in Doulting

Aldhelm is said to have been the son of Kenten or Centwine, brother of King Ine. Aldhelm quickly rose to be Abbot of Malmesbury Abbey, a post he held for over 30 years. He was a great administrator and became the first Bishop of Sherborne. More importantly he was a learned scholar, well versed in Latin poetry and Anglo-Saxon literature. He attracted many pupils and in Somerset founded a place of learning at Frome. His many works include *De Laude Virginitatis* a Latin treatise on the virtues of virginity and chastity addressed to the nuns of the double monastery at Barking, in Essex, founded in 666. Aldhelm later wrote a shorter poetic version of this treatise which was very popular. His letters are also well known: *Epistola ad Acircium* contains a treatise on the number seven and another one on metre and metrical feet for Latin poetry. He wrote many poems in Latin; one poem even describes a journey through the west of England. He also left over 100 riddles and is said to have written many poems in Anglo Saxon, but none survives though they were often turned into songs and recited in the time of King Alfred. St Aldhelm was a pioneer of Anglo Saxon literature: The Venerable Bede thought very highly of him.

On 25th May 709, whilst on a walking tour through his diocese, Aldhelm died in the church at Doulting. His body was carried to Malmesbury in Wiltshire where he was buried. The 25th May is still celebrated as his feast day. King Ine dedicated the estate to Glastonbury Abbey. Doulting is a famous quarrying area and much of the freestone was used to build Wells Cathedral and additions to Glastonbury Abbey.

To see: At Doulting there is a holy well dedicated to St Aldhelm from which springs forth the River Sheppey, which eventually runs into the River Brue. Both the parish church and the primary school in Doulting are named after St Aldhelm. There is also a magnificent early chapel set on the Purbeck clifftops in Dorset, dedicated to St Aldhelm.

Alfred 849–899

SCHOLAR, KING AND TRANSLATOR / Spent a wet winter in Athelney · Founded Athelney Abbey

Born at Wantage, Oxfordshire, Alfred was an excellent scholar who wrote several books. He laid out his legal code in *The Book of Dooms* or *Deemings*. He translated Pope

Gregory's *Pastoral Care*, *The Universal History of Orosius* and *The Ecclesiastical History of the English People* by the Venerable Bede. Alfred also made an English translation from the Latin of *The Consolations of Philosophy* by Boethius. In 878 he was trapped in the Somerset marshes around Athelney and began his guerilla campaign against the Danes, as well as undertaking a local bread-making course. Ten years later, in 888 he founded Athelney Abbey. Today Alfred is widely commemorated – there is even a baker in Glastonbury called 'Burns the Bread'.

To see: The Alfred jewel in Ashmolean Museum Oxford. The site of Athelney abbey, near East Lyng. Also a statue on Alfred's Tower near Stourhead dated 1770.

Asser died c.909 AD

MONK, SCHOLAR, TRANSLATOR AND BIOGRAPHER / Lived in Somerset

Asser was a Welsh monk who came to the court of King Alfred as a scholar and translator. He read aloud to the King and together they translated several works including Pope Gregory the Great's *Pastoral Care*. In return, Alfred gave Asser the monasteries of Congresbury and Banwell on Christmas Eve 886, along with a silk cloak and a quantity of incense "weighing as much as a stout man." Not a bad Christmas present. Asser later became Bishop of Sherborne.

In 893 Asser wrote his famous biography called *The Life of King Alfred*. Even though it is only 20,000 words long it is one of the most important sources of information on King Alfred. It is contemporary but not complete, as Alfred lived another six years. Some say it was written for a Welsh audience. The earliest copy dating from around 1100 was once owned by Leland but then became part of the Cotton Library in Westminster which was destroyed by fire in 1731. Luckily a printed version of *The Life of King Alfred* had been made in 1574 by Archbishop Parker. It is the only one to survive.

Official Speak 1: **Anglo-Saxon Chronicle**

The Anglo-Saxon Chronicle was originally compiled on the orders of King Alfred and subsequently maintained and added to by generations of anonymous scribes until the mid twelfth century. A slightly flawed but very important record of early England.

EARLY EXAMPLES RELATING TO SOMERSET:

AD 845: "This year Alderman Eanwulf, with the men of Somersetshire, and Bishop Ealstan, and Alderman Osric, with the men of Dorsetshire, fought at the mouth of the Parret with the Danish army; and there, after making a great slaughter, obtained the victory."

AD 878: "In the Easter of this year King Alfred with his little force raised a work at Athelney; from which he assailed the army, assisted by that part of Somersetshire which was nighest to it. Then, in the seventh week after Easter, he rode to Brixton by the eastern side of Selwood; and there came out to meet him all the people of Somersetshire, and Wiltshire, and that part of Hampshire which is on this side of the sea; and they rejoiced to see him. Then within one night he went from this retreat to Hey; and within one night after he proceeded to Eddington; and there fought with all the army, and put them to flight, riding after them as far as the fortress, where he remained a fortnight. Then the army gave him hostages with many oaths, that they would go out of his kingdom. They told him also, that their king would receive baptism. And they acted accordingly; for in the course of three weeks after,

He updated the Winchester version. Steinbeck lived at Redlynch near Bruton. The book was never quite finished; Steinbeck got as far as Sir Launcelot and the death of chivalry. It was only published in 1976 after Steinbeck's death. See entry for Steinbeck, page 128. By all accounts Steinbeck, who discovered Arthur in his childhood, loved his time in Somerset. Scholars have even detected Arthurian themes in several of his books including *Cup of Gold*, *Tortilla Flat*, *Of Mice and Men*, and many other writings.

The Arthurian legends, however tenuously connected to Glastonbury, are now deeply embedded in the Somerset landscape. *Le Morte d'Arthur* captured many people's minds and the myths that it wove are still very pertinent today, not least within the range of psychological archetypes. Many books about Arthur and Guinevere can also be found in the shops of Glastonbury, where they conveniently nestle alongside crystals, spirit catchers, South American weavings and dusty Tibetan Buddhas.

3 THREE WISE MEN

THESE THREE WISE MEN were incredibly influential in their day. They had a major impact on the philosophy of science and ultimately on philosophy itself. The search for empirical truth was always on their minds and laid the foundation stone for the scientific approach and ideas that today we take for granted. Locke's ideas on tolerance of religious practice are still quoted.

Adelard of Bath c.1080–1150

MATHEMATICIAN, SCIENTIST AND TRANSLATOR / Born in Bath and lived in Bath

Adelard's father Fastrad was an important tenant of Giso, Bishop of Wells. The next Bishop of Wells was John of Tours, the King's physician, who moved the episcopal seat from Wells to Bath. He may well have sent the young Adelard to Tours to complete his education. Adelard then travelled widely on the Continent and became an outstanding medieval mathematician who translated some fundamental texts from the Arabic. One of these was *The thirteen books of Euclid`s Elements of Geometry*. Originally written in Alexandria around 300 BC, *The Elements* had been translated from Greek into Arabic in the eighth century AD. No Latin version from this time has survived, so the translation was a major contribution to western science and understanding. This was cutting edge and a fundamental step in the Renaissance of science. To make the translation Adelard, who was based at Tours, went to Cordoba and disguised himself as a Muslim student. Apart from Spain he also visited Italy, Sicily, Greece and Antioch.

Other important texts he translated were *The Astronomical Tables of Al-khwarizmi* as well as treatises on astrology, the abacus and astrolabe.

He also wrote several original works of his own in letter and dialogue form to his nephew. *Quaestiones Naturales (Natural Questions), the De Eodem et Diverso (On the Same and the Different)* and a short treatise *On Birds*.

Adelard had settled back in Bath by 1122 and is known to have lived at Bath Priory. Adelard was the first European scholar of his time to venture into the world of Arabic scholarship. This was crucial not just for philosophy but for science as well. His translations were used extensively by Roger Bacon a century later.

Roger Bacon 1214–1294

PHILOSOPHER AND SCIENTIST / Born in Ilchester

Roger Bacon belonged to a family that later lost all their possesssions around Ilchester in the unsettled reign of Henry III. Bacon went to Oxford when he was 13 and developed a passion for mathematics and science. He lectured at both Oxford and Paris. Later he became a Franciscan friar and was well known as Doctor Mirabilis 'wonderful teacher'. He was attracted to the recently re-discovered works of Plato and Aristotle as well as to scientific ideas that filtered through from the Islamic world by way of Spain. Bacon then developed and advocated new theories of scientific knowledge. These theories, branching away from medieval alchemy,

astrology, superstition and dogma, placed much greater emphasis on taking down empirical evidence and using actual measurements. Bacon thus helped to lay the foundations of modern scientific method with hypotheses and objective observations.

His early works include *Opus Maius*, *Opus Minus* and *Opus Tertium*. In 1271 he wrote *Compendium Studii Philosophiae* which attacked clerical ignorance; this did not endear him to the authorities. He was constantly suspected of heresy and magic and was often placed under house arrest. He was even imprisoned by the Catholic Church in Paris for practising witchcraft and experimenting with gunpowder.

John Locke 1632–1704

PHILOSOPHER / Born Wrington, raised in Pensford

John Locke was born in his grandmother's cottage next to the north gate of Wrington church. His father was a Puritan attorney and clerk to the Justices of the Peace in Somerset. He came from Chew Magna and had served as a captain of cavalry in the Parliamentarian forces during the Civil War. On his mother's side Locke's family were Puritan tanners. John Locke grew up in Pensford and his education at Westminster School and Christ Church College, Oxford, was sponsored by Alexander Popham, who had been his father's colonel. A clear headed and original thinker, John Locke produced many interesting papers and propositions. In 1683 he fled to Holland after the Rye House Plot, using his time there very wisely. Upon his return he published some of his most famous works: an *Essay Concerning Human Understanding*, *Two Treatises of Civil Government* and *A Letter Concerning Toleration*, which are still studied today. One of the foremost philosophers of his day, he helped to kick-start the Enlightenment movement of the 18th century. His writings influenced Voltaire and Rousseau as well as David Hume, Adam Smith and the slightly rebellious Founding Fathers of the United States. His writings concerned the nature of government, money, the rise and fall of interest rates, supply and demand, and the links between property and labour, as well as the nature of self and education: ideas that certainly influenced Karl Marx. Bertrand Russell in his *History of Western Philosophy* devotes no less than 38 pages to Locke. A real tribute. John Locke was a close associate of the First Earl of Shaftesbury and like the Earl was very keen on experimenting with fruit growing. Locke died near Harlow in Essex.

To see: a statue in the porch of Wrington Church.

4 TWO HERBALISTS AND A LEG-STRETCHER

EXPLORING THE NATURAL WORLD through the properties of plants and herbs was a direct result of the Renaissance and the uncovering of classical medical texts. Many learned men, including William Turner and Henry Lyte, were keen to classify these plants and more importantly to understand their healing properties. Travellers and voyagers to foreign parts were of particular interest as they were often able to bring back new varieties to stimulate debate and research. The 'leg-stretcher' was Thomas Coryate, who walked all the way to India in 1615 but died in Surat and so never returned to Somerset.

Dr. William Turner 1508-1568

DOCTOR AND BOTANIST / Dean of Wells

William Turner is often referred to as "the Father of English botany." As a medical doctor he saw the value in taking scientific observations, applying no doubt the philosophy of Roger Bacon. He was twice Dean of Wells in 1551-1554 and again between 1560-1568 under

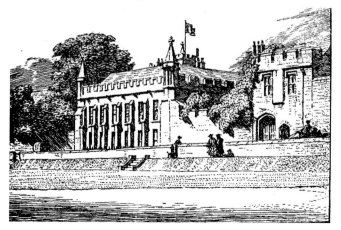

Edward VI and Elizabeth but was exiled under Mary. His *Herball* was written not in Latin but in English which was a great advance, and proved very useful to apothecaries. This predated Culpepper by about 60 years. *The Herball* gives names to many local plants which he grew in his garden at the Deanery in Wells. He advocated the therapeutic qualities of certain plants such as wormwood, feverfew and eye bright as well as the juice of the black poppy, ie opium. Turner also wrote a book on fishes and another on wine.

Henry Lyte 1529-1607

HERBALIST AND TRANSLATOR / Lived at Lytes Cary

Lytes Cary is in the parish of Charlton Mackrell, near Somerton. In 1577 Henry Lyte translated an important Dutch work, the *Cruydeboeck* of Rembert Dodoens (Antwerp, 1564) into English via the French edition. Lyte's translation of this book in 1578 was called *A Niewe Herball, or historie of plantes: wherin is contayned the whole discourse and perfect description of all sortes of herbes and plantes: their divers [and] sundry kinde.* It contains many

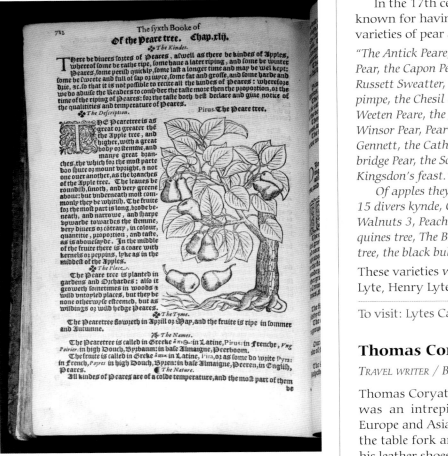

Peare illustration from page 712 of The Herball

pertinent observations and may well have been used by Shakespeare in his use of plant-lore in his plays. A copy of this book can be seen at Lytes Cary, which is now in the hands of the National Trust.

In the 17th century the garden at Lytes Cary was well known for having all possible kinds of fruit including 44 varieties of pear among them:

"The Antick Peare, the round green peare, the hundred pound Pear, the Capon Pear, the Sugar Pear, the Ruddick Pear, the Russett Sweatter, the Orrenge Peare, the Warden Pear, Pear pimpe, the Chesil or pear Nought, the Bishop's censor, the Weeten Peare, the great Kentishe Pear, the Norwich Pear, the Winsor Pear, Pear Bell, Pear Laurence, Pear Marwood, the Red Gennett, the Catherin Pear, the Bartholomew Pear, the Cary bridge Pear, the Somerton Pear an excellent pear ripe before Kingsdon's feast."

Of apples they had 'three score severall sortes, Plummes 15 divers kynde, Grapes 3 severall sortes, Cherries 1, Walnuts 3, Peaches 1, The almond tree, the Figg tree, the quines tree, The Barbary tree, the Cornishe berrie, the Philbert tree, the black bullies and the Sloe.'

These varieties were written down in 1618 by Thomas Lyte, Henry Lyte's son.

To visit: Lytes Cary, National Trust.

Thomas Coryate 1577-1617

TRAVEL WRITER / Born in Odcombe

Thomas Coryate, known as the 'Odcombe leg-stretcher' was an intrepid traveller who travelled throughout Europe and Asia on foot. He is credited with introducing the table fork and umbrella to England. For many years his leather shoes hung in Odcombe church. Today there is a carved replica of his shoes. He was one of the first travel writers; he brought back the story of William Tell and published the first version in English. Coryate belonged to the Mermaid Club, in Bread Street, London. Its members provided him with a mock passport before he

departed on his Eastern travels. He walked from Jerusalem to Agra via Turkey, Persia and Afghanistan, a distance of about 3,300 miles arriving at the Moghul court in 1615. He then travelled very widely in India and died of dysentery at Surat, in Gujerat, near an East India Company factory.

To visit: Inside Odcombe church there is a replica of Coryate's shoes carved in hamstone by Eva Harvey, 2000.

Ladyes go into the bath with garments made of a fine yellow canvas, which is stiff and made large with great sleeves like a parson's gown, the water fills it upso that it is borne off that your shape is not seen, it does not cling close as other linning… (ie linen) the gentlemen have drawers and waistcoats of the same sort of canvas.

And in 1698 she embarks on a very long journey that takes in most of the country.

On one stage she travels from Glastonbury to Taunton which is:

"16 long miles through many small places and scattering houses, through lanes full of stones and, by the great raines just before, full of wet and dirt, I passed over a large common or bottom of deep black land which is bad for the rider but good for the abider, as the proverb is, this was 2 or 3 miles long and passed and re pass'd a river as it twined about at least ten tymes over stone bridges; this river comes from Bridgewater 7 mile, the tyde come up beyond Bridgewater even within 3 mile of Taunton, its flowed by the tyde which brings up the barges with coale to this place, and having pass'd a large common which on either hand leads a great waye good riche land with ditches and willow trees all for feeding cattle, and here at this little place where boates unlade the coale, the pack horses comes and takes it in sacks and so carryes it to the places all about; this is Sea coale brought from Bristol, the horses carry 2 bushell at a tyme which at the place cost 18d and when it is brought to Taunton cost 2 shillings; the roads were full of these carriers going and returning.

Taunton is a large town having houses of all sorts of buildings both brick and stone but mostly timber and plaister; its a very neate place and looks substantial as a place of good trade; you meete all sorts of country women wrapped in manteles called West Country rockets, a large

mantle doubled together of a sort of serge, some are linstwolsey, and a deep fringe or fag at the lower end; these hang down some to their feete some only just below the wast, in summer they are in all white garments of this sort, in winter they are in red ones."

What is extraordinary is that the manuscript should have survived at all, for it was not published until 1885, with the title *Through England on a Side Saddle in the time of William and Mary*. It had by chance passed through the hands of Robert Southey the poet, who had published some of it in 1812 without knowing who had written it. This manuscript eventually came back into the hands of her family, to Lord Saye and Sele. Another well annotated edition was published in 1947 with an introduction by Christopher Morris.

Robert Sanders alias Nathaniel Spencer c.1727-1783

TRAVEL WRITER / Visited Somerset 1760s

Nathaniel Spencer was the pseudonym for a writer called Robert Sanders who was born in Perthshire. He came south, taught in various schools, worked as a hack and ended up as a compiler of Criminal Biographies serialised as *The Newgate Journal or Malefactor's Bloody Register* which ran to five volumes. He then serialised his travels across England which were published in 1771 and called *The complete English traveller, or, A new survey and description of England and Wales, containing a full account of what is curious and entertaining in the several counties, the isles of Man, Jersey, and Guernsey …* This travel guide also drew on the earlier travel writings of John Ray, Daniel Defoe, and John Pennant.

His quotations are sometimes illuminating, for they have echoes of Camden and others. He leaves pertinent

Cheddar Cliffs
near Weston-Super-Mare, Somerset

descriptions of various towns he passed through:

"The next place we visited was Langport… During the severity of the winter when the river is frozen up, the eels of which there are vast quantities, are taken in the following manner, the people approach the banks of the river, break the ice, where they think they are sheltered and pull them out with their hands. "

"At a village, called Old Cleeve, about three miles from Watchet, the people gather great quantities of sea liver wort which is found on the rocks at low water, and being cleaned and pickled, it is sent to different parts of the kingdom, and used as an excellent remedy against scurvy."

About two miles from Wiveliscombe is Milverton, a small village formerly a borough… It has four annual fairs for the sale of cattle where great numbers are bought up by London drovers. These fairs are open the Tuesday in Easter week, St James's day, the 21st July and tenth of October."

From Glastonbury we proceed to Somerton. It is chiefly remarkable for its great fairs of cattle. Near the town is an open moor or common containing some 20,000 acres where all the inhabitants have a right to feed their cattle gratis. The weekly market is on Tuesday beside which they have four annual fairs, viz Tuesday in Passion week on the Tuesday three weeks after, on the Tuesday six weeks after and on the Tuesday 9 weeks after. During these fairs it is surprising to see the vast numbers of cattle which are brought up by butchers from the principal towns in the west of England. It is distance from London 127 miles."

" Cheddar… the principal beauty of this town consists in its orchards from which they not only make great quantities of cider but also sell many loads of raw apples at neighbouring fairs. They also have vast numbers of sheep whose wool amounts to upwards of two hundred bags annually."

"At present Wincaunton is a place of considerable trade… great quantities of cheese being made in the neighbouring country, that useful article is sold to dealers who come from London."

8   BATH CHAPS

MORE THAN ANY OTHER CITY in the country, Bath has attracted writers, poets and playwrights. Some came to write and others to gawp, but all wanted to see and be seen. In the 18th and 19th century Bath was a great cauldron of ideas and exhilaration fuelled by wealth and ambitious social climbing. Many also came for their health and to take the waters. Good conversation was obligatory.

Joseph Glanvill 1636–1680

THEOLOGIAN AND PHILOSOPHER / Rector of Frome and Bath Abbey Church

Born in Plymouth, Joseph Glanvill was raised as a Puritan and educated at Oxford. In 1662 he became vicar of Frome and in 1664 he was made a Fellow of the Royal Society. In 1666 he was made rector of Bath Abbey. Glanvill was a pragmatic philosopher who sought out the middle path between conflicting ideological positions and scientific ideas. He is mainly remembered for several essays and works including *The Vanity of Dogmatising* (1661). He also argued for plain speaking and simple language when discussing scientific matters. He wrote *An Essay Concerning Preaching* as well as another essay called *The Agreement of Reason and Religion*. He was an advocate of reason and empirical knowledge hence his attitudes towards supernatural incidents. In 1666 he produced a controversial essay entitled *The Philosophical Considerations Touching the being of Witches and Witchcraft* which was written to rebut certain views of Robert Hunt, a Justice of the Peace who had persecuted witches in Somerset during the 1650s. Glanvill gathered many instances of witchcraft and believed that each event should be examined on the strength of its own evidence. Some would be found guilty, others would be found innocent. His major work on this subject called *Sadducismus Triumphatus* was published in 1681 after his death. Glanvill is buried in Bath.

Ralph Allen 1693–1764

PATRON OF THE ARTS / Lived at Prior Park

Although not a writer, Allen was a key figure in the Bath literary world at a crucial time in its development. Many poets, writers and painters were regular visitors. Some, like Fielding, even included him in their novels; he was the model for Squire Allworthy in *Tom Jones* (1749). Two years later Fielding dedicated *Amelia* to Allen. After Fielding's death Allen provided for the education of his children. Allen was also on very good terms with Alexander Pope, who became a frequent visitor from 1736. Born in Cornwall, Allen had made his money by modernising the postal system. He was also a property developer and ran several quarries at Coombe Down, using an incline railway which took the stone down to the river Avon, and gave Bath the Bath stone it so badly needed to build the Georgian city we know today. Allen built Prior Park for his own home and invited Pope to help with laying out his landscaped gardens.

To see: Prior Park.

Alexander Pope 1688-1744

POET, CRITIC AND ESSAYIST / *Often visited Bath*

Born in London, the son of a linen merchant, Pope was the author of *The Rape of the Lock* and The *Dunciad*. He had a phenomenal literary output considering he died when only 56. He was great friends with Ralph Allen and on his many visits to Bath he used to give his advice freely on how to develop the gardens and open landscape at Prior Park. He also helped to design a secret grotto for Ralph Allen's wife; it was originally encrusted with gems and rare minerals, many of them provided by the Cornish writer and geologist William Borlase. Within the grotto is also buried Mrs Allen's puppy, Miss Bounce, a Great Dane given to the couple by Pope in 1739, whose epitaph is inscribed on a stone slab in the floor.

Pope's ideas on landscape gardening are best described within an epistle he wrote to Richard Boyle, Earl of Burlington, in 1733, ideas later taken up by Capability Brown to such good effect.

"To build to plant, whatever you intend,
*   To rear the column or the arch to bend*
To swell the terrace or to sink the grot
*   In all let nature never be forgot*

But treat the goddess like a modest fair
*   Nor over dress or leave her wholly bare*
Let not each beauty everywhere be spied
*   Where half the skill is decently to hide*

He gains all points who pleasingly confounds
*   Surprises, varies and conceals the bounds.*
Consult the genius of place in all
*   That tells the water or to rise or fall."*

To see: Prior Park Landscape gardens with Palladian Bridge. The grotto is soon to be restored to its former glory.

David Hartley 1705-1757

PHILOSOPHER AND PHYSICIAN / *Lived in Bath*

Born in Halifax, Hartley trained as a doctor. He was an early advocate for the inoculation against smallpox and specialised in dissolving bladder stones. He practised in Bury St Edmonds and in London. In May 1742 the Hartleys moved 'on account of the many illnesses … which my wife has had in town' to Bath, to 'a very pleasant house in the new Square.' In Bath, Hartley pursued his calling as a physician but always kept his mind open to the philosophy of sensation. Hartley

9 17TH AND 18TH CENTURY DFLS — DOWN FROM LONDON

COMING DOWN FROM LONDON involved a journey of a few days usually taken by stage coach or post-chaise down what is now known as the A4. Some came for the season, others came for several years. It was an alternative to visiting the Continent. Bath was a place you returned to, to tell your stories. or better still, to write them.

Samuel Pepys 1633–1703

DIARIST AND CLERK TO THE NAVY BOARD / Visited Bath 1668

Born in London, Pepys went to St Paul's School and Cambridge. He worked as clerk to the Navy Board under his cousin Edward Montagu, who soon became Earl of Sandwich, First Lord of the Admiralty. Pepys secretly began his diary in 1660. In June 1668 he visited both Bath and Bristol with his wife Elizabeth, her 'mighty pretty' maid Deborah Willet with whom Pepys was infatuated, a cousin Betty Turner and his faithful Navy Office clerk, Will Hewer. Deborah came from Bristol and Pepys's wife from Bideford.

13th June Saturday *"Up at four o'clock, being by appointment called up to the Cross Bath, where we were carried one after another, myself and wife and Betty Turner, Willet and W Hewer. And by and by, though we designed to have done before company come, much company come, very fine ladies; and the manner pretty enough, only me thinks it cannot be clean to go so many bodies together in the same water. Good conversation among them that are acquainted here and stay together. Strange to see how hot the water is; and in some places though this is the most temperate Bath, the springs so hot as the feet not able to endure. But strange to see where men and women*

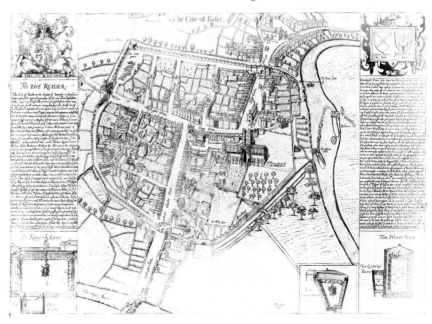

40

herein, that live all the season in the waters, that cannot but be par boiled, and look like the creatures of the bath."

They hired a coach and went to Bristol (see page 189).

William Congreve 1670–1729

PLAYWRIGHT / Visited Bath 1721 and 1722

Congreve was born in Yorkshire and educated in Dublin where he met Jonathan Swift. Congreve then entered Middle Temple and frequented the Kit Kat Club and Will's Coffee House. His best known works are: *The Old Bachelor, The Double Dealer, Love for Love, The Way of the World* and *The Mourning Bride*. He visited Bath with John Gay and John Arbuthnot. In later life Congreve suffered from gout and cataracts to his eyes.

Dr John Arbuthnot 1667–1735

SATIRIST AND PHYSICIAN / Visited Bath 1721 and 1724

A doctor and mathematician Arbuthnot was born in Kincardineshire and went to London. In 1692 he published *Of the Laws of Chance*, a translation of a book by Huygens, the first work on probability and games theory. He believed that mathematics could free the mind from superstition. He became an FRS in 1704 and physician to Queen Anne. He also became involved with Tory politics and was a founder member of the Scriblerus Club which included Jonathan Swift and Alexander Pope. Arbuthnot is credited with inspiring book III of *Gulliver's Travels* as well as Pope's *Dunciad*. It was in Bath that Arbuthnot invented the very English character of *John Bull*. It is not known whether Arbuthnot's health improved after his visits to Bath: he had kidney stones and asthma.

John Gay 1685–1732

POET AND PLAYWRIGHT. / Visited Bath 1721 and 1724

Born in Barnstaple and educated at Blundell's in Tiverton, John Gay was apprenticed to a silk mercer but soon started writing. In 1712 he became secretary to the Duchess of Monmouth and lived mostly in London. His early works include *Rural Sports* and *The Shepherd's Week*. He visited Bath in 1721 with Congreve and Arbuthnot and again in 1724. He is famous for his plays, *The Captives* (1724), the phenomenal success of *The Beggar's Opera* (1728) and its sequel *Polly* (1729). One of his patrons was William Pulteney, Earl of Bath.

Samuel Johnson 1709–1784

ESSAYIST, POET AND LEXICOGRAPHER / Visited Bath in 1776

Samuel Johnson was born in Lichfield, the son of a bookseller. He went to Oxford but left without a degree. In London he worked as a Grub Street journalist for the *Gentleman's Magazine*, wrote poetry, a play or two and then produced a biography of Richard Savage. For nine long years he immersed himself in various libraries to produce his major work *The Dictionary of the English Language*. In 1773 aged 63, Johnson paired up famously with James Boswell and visited Boswell's homeland. His acute observations are recorded in *A Journey to the Western Islands of Scotland*. Boswell left us his fine biography *The Life of Johnson*, published in 1791. Johnson was much taken with Hester Thrale, whom he knew very well in London, and later he fancied her protégé Fanny Burney.

Johnson visited them in Bath in the summer of 1776, an eventful year in American history. Boswell stayed at the Pelican. Johnson also wrote *The Vanity of Human Wishes*, the periodicals *The Rambler*, published on Tuesdays and Saturdays, *The Idler*, *The History of Rasselas, Prince of Abyssinia*, often abbreviated to *Rasselas* and the ten-volume *Lives of English Poets*.

Laurence Sterne 1713–1768

NOVELIST / Visited Bath c. 1756

Born in Clonmel in Ireland where his father was an infantry officer, Sterne was educated in Yorkshire and Cambridge. He then became a clergyman in Yorkshire at Sutton and Stillington. He visited Bath for his health (he had consumption) c.1756 and stayed at the Three Black Birds. The first volumes of *Tristram Shandy* were published in 1759. A humorous novel which had enormous influence on the genre. Sterne also wrote *A Sentimental Journey Through France and Italy*. He died in London aged 55.

Horace Walpole 1717–1797

ART HISTORIAN, NOVELIST AND MAN OF LETTERS / Visited Bath 1766

Walpole was born in London, the youngest son of Robert Walpole, the Prime Minister who 'let sleeping dogs lie'. After Eton and Cambridge, Walpole went on the Grand Tour with the poet Thomas Gray and then entered Parliament as MP for Callington. He lived in Twickenham at his home called Strawberry Hill, which gave its name to a whole neo-Gothic style in architecture. In 1754 he coined the word 'serendipity'. In 1762 he published *Anecdotes of Painting in England* and 1764 he published *The Castle of Otranto* anonymously, one of the first 'Gothic' novels. In 1766 Walpole visited Bath mainly for his health and stayed at Chapel Court and wrote about Batheaston. He also wrote *On Modern Gardening, A Description of the Villa of Mr Horace Walpole* and *Hieroglyphic*

Tales. He did not apparently return to Bath. In later life he inherited his nephew's title and became Fourth Earl of Orford.

Edmund Burke 1729–1797

AUTHOR, ORATOR AND PHILOSOPHER / Visited Bath 1753, 1756–7, 1792, 1797

Born in Dublin, the son of a solicitor, he studied at Trinity College, where he set up a debating club. He then entered the Middle Temple in London but gave up Law to travel and to write. He first visited Bath in July 1753. His first published work appeared in 1756: *A Vindication of Natural Society: A View of the Miseries Arising from Mankind*. This was the same year he visited Circus House in Bath and was treated by a Roman

Catholic doctor, Christopher Nugent. A year later, in 1757, he married the doctor's beautiful daughter, Jane Nugent. In the same year Burke published *A Philosophical Enquiry into the Origin of our Ideas of the Sublime and Beautiful* which was noticed by both Diderot and Kant. After a three year spell in Ireland, Burke became MP for Wendover in 1765, and then for Bristol in 1774. His debating skills were renowned. He wrote many pamphlets including *Reflections on the Revolution in France* (1790) which was read throughout Europe.

In September 1792 Burke stayed in Bath for two months with his wife who had accidentally overdosed on laudanum. She took the waters for nearly two months and bathed eighteen times. Burke himself had a bowel complaint. Five years later, as a very ill man, he returned to Bath in the spring and summer of 1797 to take treatment. He eventually returned to his estate at Beaconsfield and died there in July 1797.

To see: No 11 North Parade, Bath.

Oliver Goldsmith 1730–1774

Poet, novelist and playwright / Stayed in Bath 1762 and 1771

Debate still exists as to where exactly he was born; some say County Longford and others Roscommon. Even the date varies from 1728–1731, though 1730 is accepted by most. In 1744 Goldsmith went to Trinity College, Dublin, learnt to play the flute, played cards, left for Edinburgh to study medicine but eventually went busking on the Continent. Addicted to gambling, Goldsmith ended up in London and worked as an apothecary's assistant and hack writer. Here he rubbed shoulders with Samuel Johnson and Horace Walpole. He came to Bath for his health in 1762 and wrote *The Life of Richard Nash of Bath, Esquire*, ie Beau Nash. In 1771 Goldsmith stayed with his patron Lord Clare in 11 North Parade. Goldsmith is best known for his works *The Deserted Village, She Stoops to Conquer, The Vicar of Wakefield* and *Citizen of the World*. Some also believe that Goldsmith wrote *The History of Little Goody Two Shoes*. He died from a kidney complaint.

10 PIRATES AND POETS – EAST COKER'S LEGACY

Eᴀsᴛ Cᴏᴋᴇʀ is a remarkable village, for it spawned two very interesting men who made their names in quite different ways. One left, the other returned. Indeed they could hardly have been more different. The pirate and the poet, the hydrographer and the banker, the travel writer and the publisher. Both are commemorated on opposite sides of the church.

William Dampier 1651–1715

Pɪʀᴀᴛᴇ, ᴇxᴘʟᴏʀᴇʀ, ʜʏᴅʀᴏɢʀᴀᴘʜᴇʀ ᴀɴᴅ ᴡʀɪᴛᴇʀ / *Born East Coker*

Dampier was born in Hymerford House, North Coker, within the parish of East Coker and baptised in East Coker church. He was the son of George and Ann Dampier. They were tenant farmers and William received his education at the local grammar school. After his parents died he went to sea on a Weymouth trader to Newfoundland in 1669. His next voyage, 1671-2, was to Java on an East Indiaman called the *John and Martha*. Dampier served in the Dutch wars of 1673 and when convalescing was approached by his father's old landlord Squire Helyar to work on his Jamaican sugar plantation. Dampier then went to Yucatan. In 1678 he married Judith, an East Coker girl but soon afterwards became a buccaneer. In 1679 took part in the sack of Portobello, crossed the Darien isthmus and went raiding both in the Pacific and the Caribbean against Spanish ships and ports in the Bay of Campeche.

In 1683 he seized a Danish slaver off Sierra Leone, renamed her *Bachelor's Delight* and headed for the Pacific via Cape Horn. They were joined by another vessel called the *Cygnet*, under command of the aptly-named Captain

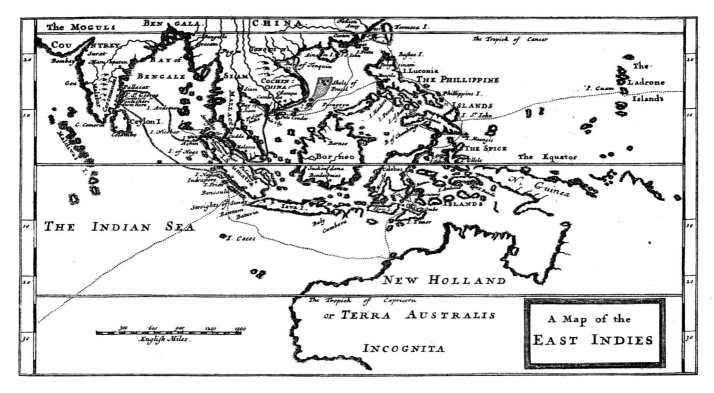

A Map of the EAST INDIES

Swan. Rations got very low and the crew mutinied and Captain Swan was put ashore at Mindanao. They sailed to Siam, China and then back again to the East Indies. In one tropical storm, in January 1688, they were driven south till they came ashore on the coast of New Holland, near the Buccaneer archipelago. They were the first Englishmen to make landfall in Australia. Dampier eventually arrived back in Deal in 1691 having been to the Nicobar Islands, Sumatra, Tonkin, Malacca, India and Capetown. Not bad for an East Coker lad.

His first book came out in 1697, *A New Voyage Round the World* and was a great success. A second volume *Voyages and Descriptions* with a section called 'Discourse on Trade winds' came out in 1699.

Dampier's books were well received by both the Royal Society and the Admiralty and he was asked to lead an expedition to New Holland, Terra Australis and New Guinea. His less than seaworthy vessel, the *Roebuck* eventually sank off Ascension Island in 1701. Dampier was a keen hydrographer and cartographer and charted parts of Western Australia and New Guinea, as well as New Hanover, New Ireland and New Britain. Today there is a Dampier archipelago near Dampier in Western Australia and Dampier straits in Papua New Guinea.

Upon his return, despite being court-martialled for maltreatment of another officer, Dampier was appointed commander of the 26-gun government ship *St George*, with a crew of 120 men. This expedition was funded by the wealthy Bristol merchants Thomas Goldney and Thomas Escott. They were joined by the 16-gun galleon called *Cinque Ports*. En-route they captured three small Spaniard ships and one vessel of 550 tons. Like the *Roebuck* the seaworthiness of the *Cinque Ports* was open to debate and there was a strong disagreement between Captain Thomas Stradling and his Scottish sailing master, Alexander Selkirk. The net result was that Alexander Selkirk was marooned at his own request on the uninhabited Chilean island of Juan Fernandez in October 1704. The clam shells Dampier brought back from this voyage can still be seen in Goldney's grotto in Clifton.

Dampier returned to England in 1707 but in 1708 was engaged again for a third circumnavigation by a privateer captain called Woodes Rogers on board *HMS Duke*. It was on this expedition with Dampier doing the navigating, that they returned to Juan Fernandez island and at last rescued Alexander Selkirk in February 1709, who had by now been marooned for four years and four months. Captain Woodes Rogers jovially referred to Selkirk as Governor of the island.

This expedition, unlike the others, had been financially successful and had accrued nearly £200,000 of profit which in today's currency is worth about £20 million. No wonder Dampier went to sea, but he never saw much of this as the funds were not shared out by Woodes Rogers till 1719, four years after Dampier's

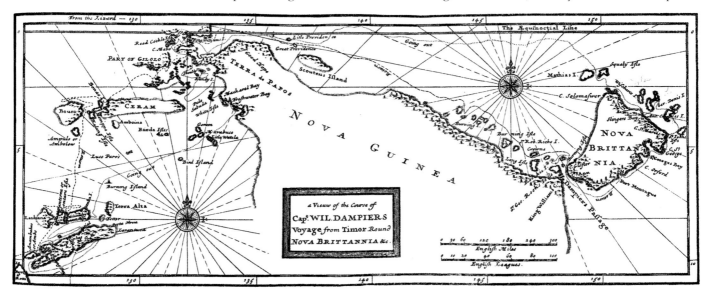

Fishes taken on the Coast of New Guinea

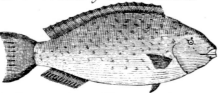

This Fish fins & tail are blew on ỹ edges & red in the middle with blew spots all over ỹ Body, but ỹ Belly white.

A Pike Fish Conger on ỹ Coast of New Guinea

This Fish is a pale red with blew spots on ỹ body the long Tail blew in ỹ midle & white on ỹ side.

death. In the meantime Dampier had produced a third book called *Continuation of a Voyage to New Holland* which came out in 1709. Dampier never published an account of this, his third voyage around the world, but Woodes Rogers did. Parts of his book called *A Cruising Voyage Round the World* may well have been contributed to by Dampier, who was by now living in London but not in good health.

Alexander Selkirk's experiences later became the inspiration for the novel *Robinson Crusoe* by Daniel Defoe, first published in 1719. Defoe was supposed to have met Selkirk in the Llandoger Trow, an Inn near Welsh Back in Bristol docks. As it happens Captain Woodes Rogers lived nearby in 33-35 Queen's Square, and both Dampier and Defoe were frequent visitors.

Dampier's literary and scientific legacy was very important indeed. His observations and writings influenced Alexander von Humboldt, Charles Darwin and Joseph Bankes. Dampier was however unfairly parodied by Jonathan Swift in *Gulliver's Travels*.

There is some question whether or not Swift and Defoe helped Dampier to re-write his journals. In the original account of the 'savages' on the Australian coast (the aboriginals) Dampier admired their ability to survive in such harsh and dry conditions. Samuel Taylor Coleridge also had a great respect for Dampier, referring to him as: "old Dampier, a rough sailor, but a man of exquisite mind".

An interesting footnote is that a mariner called Simon Hatley sailed with Dampier in 1703-05 and again with Woodes Rogers and Dampier in 1708-09. Hatley was captured by the Spanish and imprisoned in Lima. He went out again, this third time with another Bristol captain, Captain Shelvocke and in a fit of pique when hampered by bad weather and unfavourable winds,

Hatley shot a black albatross when they were to the west of Cape Horn. This event was recorded in a book by Shelvocke published in 1726. *A Voyage Round The World by Way of the Great South Sea* and mentioned Hatley's deed.

F.3.

A Noddy. of N. Holland. P.85&99.

F.5.

The head & greatest part of ÿ neck of this bird is red. & therein differs from the Avosetta of Italy.

A Comon Noddy. P 99.

F. 6.

F. 4.

The Bill & Leggs of this Bird are of a Bright Red.

We all observed, that we had not the sight of one fish of any kind, since we were come to the Southward of the streights of le Mair, nor one sea-bird, except a disconsolate black Albatross, who accompanied us for several days (...), till Hattley, (my second Captain) observing, in one of his melancholy fits, that this bird was always hovering near us, imagin'd, from his colour, that it might be some ill omen. (...) He, after some fruitless attempts, at length, shot the Albatross, not doubting we should have a fair wind after it.

This story was circulating around Bristol for many years before it was picked up by Coleridge in Nether Stowey. So these mariner's accounts of voyages which were in debt to Dampier's navigation, eventually led to great works of literature. (See Woodes Rogers and Shelvocke pages 189-192).

It is a curious and pertinent fact that William Dampier and Andrew Eliot Junior should have been born in the same year, 1651 and in the same parish, East Coker, and both left the parish to go overseas in the same year 1669. They would have undoubtedly have known each other well. One sailed three times round the world and survived countless storms and the other drowned off Massachusetts. It may well be that the line from *East Coker* 'old men should be explorers' is a reference to William Dampier.. or at least an unfulfilled wish of Eliot's in old age.

To see: There is a brass plaque to Dampier in East Coker Church and clam shells in Goldney House Grotto, Clifton.

T. S. Eliot 1888-1965

Poet, banker, playwright and publisher / Ashes interred East Coker Church

Acres have been written about T. S. Eliot, whole forests have been chopped down in the service of literary criticism analysing his work in minute detail, a veritable growth industry. Student essays alone must have accounted for half of Finland by now. But East Coker has a special place in his life. Not only was the second of the *Four Quartets* named after East Coker but the poet's ashes are safely interred in the church behind a memorial plaque.

In many senses T. S. Eliot was coming home at last. In the middle of the turbulent seventeenth century, Eliot's ancestors had emigrated from East Coker to America. In 1669 they sailed to Massachusetts and settled in a small coastal community called Beverly near Cape Ann. *"In my beginning is my end. In my end is my beginning"* are the poignant first and last lines of the poem *East Coker* which is loosely based on the village. Eliot uses the village as a metaphor for a meditation on time. The poem ponders the depths of Christian mysticism, biblical time and regeneration. Eliot examines language and philosophy, history and spirit of place and in the process finds a meaning within Buddhist teachings and pragmatic wisdom. Eliot considered the *Four Quartets* to be his masterpiece and this work led directly to the award of the Nobel Prize for literature in 1948. The *Four Quartets* were also based on the four elements. The first, *Burnt Norton* symbolised air; *East Coker* was earth; *The Dry Salvages*, water and *Little Gidding*, fire.

Eliot first visited East Coker in 1936/7. Why he did not revisit more often is not clear but there was a rumour that he might have retired there. Possibly it was too far

Porlock Bay

Exmoor

Oure

N: Purlock
Almersworthy
Culbone
Minehead
Luccomb
Dunster
Wotton Courtney
Stoke Pero
Timbercomb

CARHAMTON HVND
Carenton
or Carhampton
Withicomb
S Ducumans at:
S Decombs
Old Clene
Williton
Watchet
EastQu
Donyfe
West
Orchard
Samford
Bret

Exford
Cutcomb
Luxborough
Nettlecomb
Leighland
MonkSilver
Bick
Stoke
Elworthy

Winesford
Wethipole
Exton
Wethihill
Treborough
WILLITON

Haukridge
Brupton Regis
Vpton
HUND
Brupton
Clatworthy
Ralph
Tolland
Lidi

Tuchen
Molland
W Ansty
E Ansty
Bare Linch
Dulverton
Haddon Beacon
Hewish
Champstover
Chipstable
N CURRY
Wivelscomb
Fitshe

Comb
Bustford
Langridg
Higley
Morbath
Exbridg
Bampton
Bittescomb
Skilgat
Raddington
Petton
Dipford
Clayhanger
Milverton
Ok

MILVERTON
Stanleigh or Stowley
Badleston
Kittesford
Langford
Runton
Mi

PART

Ex R

Ashrittell
HVND
Margrets
thurn
San
Holcomb

Map by
Robert Morden
from Camden's
Britannia 1695

PART TWO

FROM NETHER STOWEY TO COMBE FLOREY

From Romantic poetry to Waugh

11 THE ROMANTIC LOT SWANNING AROUND THE QUANTOCK

T HE ROMANTIC POETS are so well known that there is little to add except perhaps that without opium, Somerset cider and the coastal air, Coleridge's imagination might not have been so vivid. What is also pertinent is that Coleridge often relied on other people's accounts to trigger his imagination, for example Samuel Purchas's *Pilgrimage* and the accounts of mariners: Dampier, Woodes Rogers and Shelvocke. Interestingly Thomas De Quincey first met Coleridge in a street in Bridgwater outside a coaching inn and it is from De Quincey's later writings that we learn most about the poets.

Samuel Taylor Coleridge 1772-1834

POET / Lived at Nether Stowey

Born in Ottery St Mary, the youngest of ten children, Samuel Coleridge's father was vicar and master of the local school. After Cambridge, meeting with Robert Southey, and marriage to Sara Fricker in Bristol, Coleridge had his honeymoon in Clevedon. (See STC in Clevedon page 178) He then moved down to Nether Stowey in 1796 on the insistence of the local tanner Tom Poole, who not only gave them a rent-free house, but paid off his debts. Saint indeed, the snuff-taking tanner. In June 1797, after preaching one Sunday at the Unitarian Church in Bridgwater, Coleridge walked 40 miles to Racedown in Dorset to stay with William and his sister Dorothy Wordsworth. They got on famously. The rest is history, or should I say poetry.

Dorothy Wordsworth has left us this fine description of Coleridge:

"At first I thought him plain, that is for about three minutes: he is pale and thin, has a wide mouth, thick lips and not very good teeth, longish loose-growing half-curling rough black hair. But if you hear him speak five minutes you think no more of them. His eye is large and full, not dark but grey; such an eye as would receive from a heavy soul the dullest expression; but it speaks every emotion of his animated mind."

The Wordsworths, who were staying rent-free at Racedown, later moved into Alfoxden near Kilve where they did pay some rent. Coleridge sent a carriage over to collect their belongings. After a year, however, their lease on Alfoxden was not renewed. The dynamic bond between Coleridge, William Wordsworth and his sister Dorothy was very creative and out of this period together many poems flowed, notably: *The Ancient Mariner, Frost at Midnight*, the first part of *Christabel* and all the other wonderful poems from the *Lyrical Ballads*. It was a heady, sometimes opium-and-cider induced Somerset landscape that inspired them.

A creative period that drew in other admirers. Coleridge, when denied a walk, by having had boiling milk spilt on his foot by Sara, his overworked wife, produced *This Lime-Tree Bower My Prison*. He was visited by the essayists Lamb and Hazlitt. Dorothy began writing her journal at Alfoxden. Their habits were so strange and outlandish that their walks at night eventually aroused much curiosity. They were even mistaken for French spies.

In autumn 1797 Coleridge walked from Porlock Weir to the church at Culbone - a steep climb, but it was a landscape that he knew well. His mother was the daughter of an Exmoor farmer and some of her family had come from the Porlock area. Tradition has it that Coleridge stayed at Ash Farm, where he holed up with his three grains of opium for dysentery or other indispositions and wrote the first part of *Kubla Khan*. The fact of the matter was that he had a copy of a much earlier book open on his knee, called *Purchas his Pilgrimage*, from 1614, which is about the same time that Thomas Coryate was in India. (See Odcombe Leg-stretcher, page 20) Purchas's book even contains the lines:

> In *Xamdu* did *Cublai Can* build a stately Palace, encompassing sixteen *miles* of plaine *ground* with a *wall*, wherein are *fertile* Meddowes, pleasant springs, *delightfull* Streames, and all sorts of beasts of chase and game, and *in the middest* thereof a sumptuous house of *pleasure*, which may be removed from place to place.
>
> PURCHAS HIS PILGRIMAGE, p. 472

This became in Coleridge's mind:

> *In Xanadu did Kubla Khan*
> *A stately pleasure-dome decree:*
> *Where Alph, the sacred river, ran*
> *Through caverns measureless to man*
> *Down to a sunless sea.*
>
> *So twice five miles of fertile ground*
> *With walls and towers were girdled round:*
> *And there were gardens bright with sinuous rills,*
> *Where blossomed many an incense-bearing tree;*
> *And here were forests ancient as the hills,*
> *Enfolding sunny spots of greenery.*

It has been surmised that 'caverns measureless to man' were none other than Cheddar gorge, which Coleridge had visited with Southey, and 'the sunless sea' the sea off North and West Somerset, which does at times have a certain murky look to it….Samuel Purchas c.1575-1626, was a geographer, travel writer and contemporary of Richard Hakluyt. See page 186. It is said that Coleridge borrowed the Purchas book from Wordsworth and took it with him on his quest for a vision. A vision that was sadly interrupted by the gentleman from Porlock…

The other masterpiece written by Coleridge during this time in Somerset was *The Rime of the Ancient Mariner*. One of Coleridge's neighbours, John Cruickshank, had a nightmare about a spectre ship. This, combined with details from works relating to Shelvocke and Dampier, gave Coleridge the rest of the story, with a little help from his new friends William and Dorothy. The idea of shooting an albatross comes from the real shooting of a black albatross near Cape Horn on one of the voyages associated with Shelvocke by a man called Simon Hatley. He was on board the *Speedwell* when they were beset by storms and waited for better weather to round Cape Horn. Hatley thought that the black albatross was associated with the devil, it dogged them and brought them bad luck. Hatley had already sailed with Dampier and Woodes Rogers and was well aware of the dangers of sinking or being marooned. See William Dampier, Woodes Rogers and Shelvocke pages 46-50.

The port of Watchet played its part: from there the ancient mariner sets out on his voyage and it is to Watchet that he returns with his tale of woe. The outline of the story was discussed there by Coleridge and Wordsworth. Today there is a statue by the harbour of the emaciated Ancient Mariner weighed down by the large albatross.

In September 1798 Coleridge went to Germany with the Wordsworths and in the autumn of 1799 Coleridge went to visit them in County Durham. He promptly fell in love with William's sister-in-law, Sara Hutchinson. He visited the Lake District with the Wordsworths and moved with his family to Keswick. He returned to visit Tom Poole in Nether Stowey in 1801 and 1803. His last visit there was in 1807 when he met the young Thomas De Quincey in Bridgwater outside the Chubb's house. De Quincey later documented the Lakeland poets; he was not always flattering. The opium had got to them and to him by that stage. In the end Coleridge lived out the last 18 years of his life in London, under the care of Dr Gillman in Highgate. Samuel Taylor Coleridge was one of the most remarkable poets to have ever lived in Somerset, and it was the inner and outer landscape that fired his imagination. While he was in Somerset he produced two of the most memorable and popular poems in the English language.

To visit: Nether Stowey: National Trust Cottage in Lime Street is open to the public. Watchet: a modern statue of the Ancient Mariner on quayside. Culbone Church and walk The Coleridge Trail on the Quantocks.

Also see the film *Pandemonium* made by Julien Temple in 2001. It charts the lively and enigmatic relationships between Coleridge (Linus Roache), Wordsworth (John Hannah) and his dynamic sister Dorothy (Emily Woof) and Sarah Coleridge (Samantha Morton).

William Wordsworth 1770-1850

Poet / Lived at Alfoxden, between Holford and Kilve, 1797-98

William was born in Cockermouth, Cumberland. His father was a legal factotum for Lord Lowther and had a large house to go with the job. William had three brothers, Richard, John and Christopher and one sister, Dorothy. In 1778 William was separated from his sister and did not see her for nine years. Their mother died in 1779 and their father in 1783. William went to Cambridge and in 1788 wrote his first poem *An Evening Walk*. He then returned to Penrith to see Dorothy and her friend Mary Hutchinson whom he was to marry many years later. In 1790 he walked over 2000 miles across revolutionary France to get to the Alps, crossed them and went to Lake Como and then returned via the Rhine. An adventurous trip for those days. He returned to France in 1791, visited the sights in Paris, met some of the Jacobins and then went to Orleans, where he fell in love with Annette Vallon, the daughter of a Royalist surgeon. She became pregnant and he did a runner just as the September massacres of 1792 began. He stayed six weeks in Paris observing the sharp workings of the revolutionary machine and just as his daughter was born he flipped back to England.

On February 1st 1793 France declared war on England, a war which with one intermission in 1802, was to last for 22 years. He went on various walking tours notably to Salisbury Plain and a visit to the Wye valley. In January 1795 a friend from Cumberland, Raisley Calvert, died of consumption and left William the sum of £900. A neat sum for a poor aspiring poet. William was offered the use of Racedown Lodge in West Dorset by John and Azariah Pinney, whose father John Pinney lived in Bristol. It was in his house in 7 Great George Street, that Wordsworth first met Coleridge, Southey and Joseph Cottle.

With his beloved sister Dorothy, William set up home and they were paid £50 a year to look after the young son of a friend, Basil Montagu. This sojourn at Racedown was one of their happiest times. They had the house rent free to themselves for two years. William was, however, a bit depressed at leaving his new but secret family in France and the way things were going on the other side of the Channel did not bode well. Dorothy therefore used all her charms to bring him back to earth and cajoled him into writing poetry again. *Evening Walk* had in fact been written with her in mind in 1788.

Racedown had an excellent library. Mary Hutchinson came to stay for six months. They walked and talked and grew vegetables. They had dropped out and enjoyed it. William once rode to Lyme Regis to order coal but absentmindedly left the horse tied up and had to go back to get it the next day. Whilst at Racedown Wordsworth experimented with writing a blank verse tragedy called *The Borderers* and worked on his Salisbury Plain poem.

In March 1797 Wordsworth called on Coleridge in Nether Stowey and read him *The Ruined Cottage*. Interestingly both Coleridge and Wordsworth were influenced by a long descriptive poem called *Lewesdon Hill*, written in 1788 by a local vicar called William Crowe of Stoke Abbot. Crowe's poem was about the very landscape that they were walking over and one or two phrases creep into a later, now famous poem by Wordsworth: *Lines written a few miles above Tinterne Abbey* published in 1798. The real influence of the poem *Lewesdon Hill* on both Coleridge and Wordsworth has recently been assessed in an essay by Catherine Simmonds.

A few months later, on June 5th 1797, Coleridge returned the call and stayed at Racedown for two weeks.

with detailed accounts of visits to South Molton, Bath, Bristol and London. His first entry is very revealing indeed; he was observing The Romantics very closely, and in so doing recorded for posterity their antics:

"Wed October 23rd 1799 Went with my wife to Stowey and she bought a gown of Mr Frank Poole who smiled and bowed graciously. Saw that Democratic hoyden Mrs Coleridge who looked so like a friskey girl or something worse that I was not surprised that a Democratic libertine should choose her for a wife. The husband gone to London suddenly. No one here can tell why…"

12 BIRDS OF PASSAGE

Some of these women writers are very well known but there are many others who deserve a wider audience. They often battled against male prejudice and the strictures of being either single or, indeed, married.

Elizabeth Rowe 1674-1737

POET AND NOVELIST / Born in Ilchester · Lived in Frome

Her father, Walter Singer, was a disssenting minister who had been imprisoned in Ilchester Jail during Charles II's reign, as were so many of them in Somerset. He met his wife when she visited the prison. Walter later became a wealthy clothier and moved to Eggford Farm near Frome. There Elizabeth became acquainted with Henry Thynne, the son of Viscount Weymouth of Longleat. He taught her Italian, French and Latin. Elizabeth began writing at the age of twelve and by 1693 she was contributing poetry to the *Athenian Mercury* under the pen names of *Philomela* and *Pindarick Lady*. Many of these were published in 1696, in a collection called *Poems on Several Occasions*. In 1709 she published *A Collection of Divine Hymns and Poems*. A year later she married the poet and biographer Thomas Rowe whom she had met in Bath. He was thirteen years her junior. They moved to Hampstead, but he died of consumption in 1715 aged only 28. His eight biographies were published posthumously. Elizabeth returned to Frome and there she wrote elegies to her dead husband which were much admired by Pope, and a series of novellas in letter form, *Friendship in Death: in Twenty Letters from the Dead to the Living* as well as *Letters Moral and Entertaining*. *The History of Joseph* in eight volumes appeared in 1736. Her letters were very popular and held in high regard as models of moral prose.

Her works were translated into German and French. Her last volume of poetry was published in 1739. Elizabeth Rowe died of apoplexy and was buried in her father's grave at Rook Lane Congregational Church in Frome.

Catherine Macaulay 1731-1791

HISTORIAN / Lived in Bath 1774-1779

Born in Kent, Catherine Macaulay was a rare talent, a feminine historian and political activist, who sympathised with both the French and American Revolutions. She moved to Bath in 1774 and took a house in St James's Parade and then moved to 2 Alfred Street. She produced an eight-volume *History of England from the Accession of James I to the Elevation of the House of Hanover*. She wrote it between 1763-83. Horace Walpole regarded it as superior to Hume, a rare compliment. She also wrote many political and philosophical essays and pamphlets, two of which challenged the ideas of no lesser mortal than Edmund Burke. In 1783 she wrote her *Treatise on the Immutability of Moral Truth* and another important work in 1790 on education: *Letters on Education with Observations on Religious and Metaphysical Subjects*. Catherine Macaulay was also a friend of Dr Johnson. She had a scandalous marriage to William Graham in 1778. She was 66, and he was a 21 year old surgeon's mate. She left Bath.

Jane Austen 1775-1817

NOVELIST / Lived in Bath 1801-1806

Jane Austen was born in Steventon, Hampshire, where her father was rector. Her mother Cassandra came from the Leigh family of Stoneleigh in Warwickshire. Jane Austen lived in Bath 1801-1806 before going to live in Clifton, which she appeared to prefer. Jane Austen is best known as author of *Pride and Prejudice, Sense and Sensibility, Mansfield Park* and *Emma*. Her biographer Claire Tomalin regards her early work *Lady Susan* as a remarkable piece of writing for a young woman of 21. It was in Bath that Jane Austen worked on *Lady Susan*. It takes the form of an exchange of 41 letters. The main characters are Sir Reginald de Courcy and his son, and Lady Susan Vernon a racy 35 year old widow and her 16 year old daughter Frederica. The letters are well worth reading. It was not considered suitable for the drawing rooms of Bath and was only published in 1871.

She also worked on another novel called *The Watsons* about an invalid clergyman with four unmarried daughters. Her father became ill whilst living there and died in 1805. Two of Jane Austen's novels, *Northanger Abbey* and *Persuasion*, are largely set in Bath. Her two brothers Charles and Francis Austen, both served in the Navy during the Napoleonic War. She gleaned all sorts of useful details from them for her novels, about prize money, young dashing officers and crusty admirals on half pay. Her brother Henry was her literary agent. None of her four novels published in her lifetime bore her name. Jane later moved back to Hampshire and lived in the village of Chawton. She is buried in Winchester Cathedral.

When she was a child Jane often stayed with her aunt and uncle at 1, The Paragon in Bath, and with Edward Austen and his family at No 13, Queen Square. In 1801 the Austen family lived for three years at 4 Sydney Place, then moved to 27 Green Park Buildings, 25 Gay Street and finally to Trim Street in 1806. Jane's father is buried in St Swithin's, Walcot, where he and Cassandra Leigh had been married on 26th April, 1764. There is now a Jane Austen Centre at 40 Gay Street.

Mary Shelley 1797-1851

NOVELIST / Lived in Bath

Born in London, Mary Wollstonecraft Godwin was the daughter of the political philosopher William Godwin. Her mother Mary Wollstonecraft was also a philosopher and novelist. She wrote *A Vindication of the Rights of Woman: with Strictures on Political and Moral Subjects* as well as a history of the French Revolution. She died 11 days after her daughter Mary was born.

In 1812, aged only 15, Mary first met the poet Percy Bysshe Shelley, who was already married. A year or two later they famously fell in love and they would meet at her mother's graveside in St Pancras. In 1814 Percy abandoned his wife Harriet, and the young lovers then eloped to the Continent, with Mary's step-sister Claire Clairmont, in tow. They reached Switzerland, but returned six weeks later in September 1814. Mary was already pregnant and penniless. A daughter was born in London in February 1815 but died twelve days later. That year Percy's grandfather left him an annual income of £1,000, so they set up home in Bishopsgate. In January

1816 Mary Godwin gave birth to a son called William.

In 1816, the couple famously spent a summer with Lord Byron, John William Polidori and Claire Clairmont near Geneva, in Switzerland. Claire was pregnant with Lord Byron's daughter which added another layer of complexity. It was here that Mary Godwin, as she was still called, conceived the idea for her novel *Frankenstein*, one dark and stormy night in June they held a contest to make up the best horror story. As it happens, two years previously, in 1814, Mary and Percy had been to a lecture by Andrew Crosse in London (see Crosse pages 68-69). Mary had also heard a lot about Crosse's experiments from Robert Southey.

When they returned home in September 1816 they moved to Bath, to conceal Claire's pregnacy from Mary's father, William Godwin. They set up home in 5 Abbey Churchyard with the editor of the *Bath Herald*. They also lived at 4 Roman Pavement and 6 Queen Square. Mrs Clairmont was living nearby at Mrs Gilbert's rooming-

house in 12 New Bond St Idyllic, you might think - but then things suddenly took a strange turn for the worse. In October 1816 Fanny Imlay, Mary's half sister killed herself in Swansea with an overdose of laudanum. She had been in love with Percy a year or two before and wanted to live with them, as Claire had done, but this was refused. Then in December there was a second tragedy: Harriet, Percy's estranged wife, drowned herself in the Serpentine. Mary Godwin and Percy Shelley wasted no time in getting married. In January 1817 Claire gave birth to Lord Byron's child.

In March 1817 Mary Shelley moved from Bath to Marlow on the Thames and finished *Frankenstein* in May. The book was published anonymously in January 1818. Mary Shelley therefore must have written a fair chunk of *Frankenstein* whilst living in Bath.

Emma Marshall 1828-1899

Novelist / Lived in Clifton, Wells and Weston-super-Mare

Born in Norfolk, Emma's family moved to Clifton in about 1849 and came to know John Addington Symonds (see page 198). She corresponded with the American poet Longfellow. Emma married Hugh Marshall, a clerk in the West of England Bank. In 1855 they moved to Wells, where he became the bank manager. They lived there for twelve idyllic years in what is now the National Trust Shop in the Market Place. She had seven of her nine children there. She also started writing novels. Her first book was called *Happy Days at Fernbank*. Another one was about Bishop Thomas Ken and several others were set in the Mendips. In 1869 they moved to Exeter, then to Gloucester.

Disaster struck in 1878 when her husband lost his job. The bank failed and they had large debts from the liability of their bank shares. They moved into lodgings in Weston-super-Mare. Emma swung into action and saved the day by writing books such as *Lady Alice* and *Eastwood Ho!* She worked hard for twenty years as a writer to clear those debts, writing historical romances such as *Memories of Troublous Times*, *Under Salisbury Spire* and *Penshurst Castle*. In the 1880s they all moved back to Bristol. She was always keen to use real locations and local history. One such book was called *Bristol Diamonds*,

13 EMINENT AND ECCENTRIC – CLERGYMEN

S OME CLERGYMEN were eminent, others were eccentric. The most entertaining was Sydney Smith, who was both eminent and eccentric. One was obsessed with cider, one prepared Monmouth for execution, another was sold for 25/- and then walked naked across Afghanistan and a fourth committed suicide. Many kept diaries about themselves and their parishioners.

Thomas Beckington 1390-1465

BISHOP AND TRAVEL WRITER / Born in Beckington, buried in Wells

Thomas Beckington, the son of a weaver, was educated at Winchester and New College, Oxford. An assiduous clerk, he rose through the ranks to serve under Duke Humphrey of Gloucester (who founded the Bodleian Library). Beckington eventually became the Secretary to Henry VI and Lord Privy Seal. He left journals in Latin from his travels and peace negotiations in France, mainly around Calais and in Armagnac. He also left many writings in the Privy Council records and gave legal advice to Henry VI in 1440 when the King founded Eton College. Three years later Thomas Beckington was made Bishop of Bath and Wells and his resplendent effigy can be seen in Wells Cathedral and his bishop's ring is in the cathedral library.

Thomas Chaundler c.1417–1490

CHANCELLOR OF OXFORD UNIVERSITY AND PLAYWRIGHT / Born in Wells

Thomas Chaundler grew up in Wells and went to Winchester and New College, Oxford. He studied law and theology. His patron was Thomas Beckington, Bishop of Bath and Wells, who made him Chancellor of Wells Cathedral in 1452. He was also Warden of New College and became Chancellor of Oxford University in 1457, a post he held for four years and again in 1472 for another seven years, both at important times in the life of the University.

Chaundler also wrote several plays, one called *Liber Apologeticus de Omni Statu Humanae Naturae*, (A defence of human nature in every state), an academic drama in Latin and a morality play which was written for Thomas Beckington. It was accompanied by fifteen fine illustrations drawn by a Burgundian artist. Chaundler also wrote *Libellus de Laudibus Duarum Civitatum*, a debate in poetry which was presented to Beckington. Chaundler eventually retired from academic life and was made honorary chaplain to Edward IV and Dean of Hereford, where he died in 1490. He is buried in Hereford Cathedral.

Rev John Beale 1608–1683

Scientist, author and orchardist / Vicar of Yeovil 1660 –1683

John Beale was a gifted writer, scientific observer, orchard fanatic and Fellow of the Royal Society. He was a great friend of John Evelyn and the Phelips family at Montacute. He contributed 57 *Aphorisms on Cider* to Evelyn's *Pomona* published in 1664. He was a noted cider enthusiast and scientific commentator who corresponded weekly with Samuel Hartlib. In 1657 Beale wrote *Herefordshire Orchards – A Treatise on Fruit Trees*, containing valuable sections on cider, perry, and English vineyards. From as early as 1638, Beale had the living at Sock Dennis near Ilchester and thus was able to document the production of bottle-fermented sparkling cider at Montacute House. He was also chaplain to Charles II. So keen was Beale on orchards that he bore the cost of distributing 20,000 grafts of Herefordshire Redstreak, Genet Moyle apples and Barland pears to growers in Somerset, Devon, and Dorset.

Thomas Ken 1637–1711

Bishop of Bath and Wells / Buried in Frome

Born in Little Berkhamstead, Bishop Ken was a quiet, learned cleric of strong principles and great courage. His father was a London lawyer; his mother the daughter of a poet called John Chalkhill. Ken's half-sister Anne was married to Izaak Walton, author of *The Compleat Angler*. Ken was educated at Winchester and New College Oxford, where he met George Hooper and Thomas Thynne. Ordained in 1663, he was later made a Prebend of Winchester Cathedral. In 1679, he was sent to the Hague to succeed George Hooper as chaplain to Princess Mary, wife of the future William III, whose treatment of his

wife caused Ken to rebuke him. Charles II later made Ken his own chaplain and was heard to say ruefully, "I must go and hear Little Ken tell me of my sins".

But Thomas Ken was no push-over. When Charles descended with his court on Winchester, he tried to billet Nell Gwynne on Ken - who refused to have her under his roof. But when in 1684, the bishopric of Bath and Wells fell vacant, King Charles said, "Who shall have Bath and

Wells but that little dark fellow who would not give poor Nelly a lodging?" Thomas Ken also went to Tangier and dined with Pepys.

In July 1685, during the Monmouth Rebellion, the rebels marched into Wells, stabled horses in the cathedral, smashed glass and discharged their muskets at the West Front statues. After the battle of Sedgemoor, Ken prepared the Duke of Monmouth for his execution in the Tower of London and accompanied him to the scaffold. After the botched execution Ken rode back to Somerset and tended wounded prisoners crammed into the cathedral cloisters. As Bishop he lived humbly and every Sunday dined 12 poor men and women in the Palace. He also rode all over Somerset to visit its villagers; wrote *Practice of Divine Love* and a manual of prayers for those taking the waters at Bath.

In 1688 Ken and six other bishops stopped James II from having his Declaration of Indulgence read in all churches - thus bypassing Parliament. Tried for seditious libel and kept in the Tower with execution in prospect, the seven bishops were later acquitted amid great rejoicing. That autumn James II fled and William and Mary were brought over from Holland. But Ken would not take the oath to support King William. In 1691 he was forced out of his bishopric and spent the rest of his life living at Longleat, thanks to his old friend Thomas Thynne. In 1704 George Hooper became Bishop of Bath and Wells. When he died Ken was buried, "in the churchyard of the nearest parish under the east window of the church, just at sunrising". This church was St John the Baptist in Frome.

To see: His monument and altar cross, St John's, Frome; his dining table and portrait, the Bishop's Palace, Wells, see also page 167 for his hymns.

Richard Alleine 1610-1681

Puritan Divine and author / Born at Ditcheat

Alleine was educated at Oxford. He was a Puritan writer seized by the Divine spirit who became rector of Batcombe in 1641. He was very controversial and during the Commonwealth period helped Parliamentarian forces with the expulsion of ministers that did not meet with the approval of the new regime. After the Restoration he was himself ejected in 1662. Under the Five Mile Act passed in 1665, ministers were forbidden to return within five miles of their former parishes. Alleine went to Frome Selwood and preached there. His *Vindiciae Pietatis* (1660) was seized by Roger Norton, the Royal printer, and taken to the Royal kitchens to be burnt. Some pages were saved, bound up and sold, then seized again and 'bisked', that is painted over in ink with a brush, and returned to the kitchens to fuel the Royal fires. The book was later reissued with additions as *The Godly Man's Portion* in 1663, *Heaven Opened* in 1666, *The World Conquered* in 1668. Alleine also produced such works as *The Best of Remedies for the Worst of Maladies* and *A Rebuke to Backsliders*, and a *Spurr for Loyterers*. John Wesley later credited him with writing the covenant prayer that was introduced into Methodism in 1755 and gave the movement its spiritual backbone.

Joseph Alleine 1634-1668

Puritan author / Lived in Taunton and Wellington. Buried in Taunton

Born in Devizes, Joseph Alleine was a Nonconformist vicar and Puritan author. A highly intelligent man, he was educated at Oxford. In 1655 he was working as an assistant to George Newton of St Mary Magdalene, Taunton. Keeping it in the family, he married his cousin Theodosia Alleine (1654-1677) who was born at Batcombe, daughter of Richard Alleine. Joseph wrote many popular works such as *Divers Practical Cases of Conscience Satisfactorily Resolved* and *The True Way to happiness*. Like many Nonconformist preachers he was ejected during the Restoration in 1662 and was supposed to abide by the Five Mile Rule. He was thrown into prison in Ilchester at least twice for preaching and even wrote *Letters from a Prison* whilst there. He was tried in Taunton Castle, found not guilty but still fined 100 marks (which he refused to pay) and then promptly sent back to prison. Eventually he was released in 1664 and then moved to Wellington, and then back towards Taunton to a house called Fullands. Being harassed continually for preaching, his health declined and Alleine took the waters in Bath, where he died aged only 34. 'If I should die fifty miles away, let me be buried at Taunton,' and he was. His wife Theodosia wrote a compilation called *The Life and Death of Mr. Joseph Alleine*, published in 1672. Amazingly Joseph Alleine's work is still in print. *An Alarm to the Unconverted* was published posthumously in 1671 and sold 20,000 copies. Twenty years later, when it was renamed *A Sure Guide to Heaven*, a further 50,000 copies were sold. Useful reading in a recession.

Parson James Woodforde 1740-1803

Diarist and food commentator / Born Ansford, Castle Cary
See Diarists etc page 152

Parson William Holland 1746-1819

Diarist / Lived in Over Stowey see page 69

Rev John Skinner 1772-1839

DIARIST AND ANTIQUARIAN / Born at Claverton, lived at Camerton

John Skinner went to Cambridge. He was destined to become a lawyer but ended up a curate at Brent Knoll. He became Rector of Camerton in 1800, a post he held for nearly 40 years. An amateur antiquarian and archaeologist in the mode of William Stukeley, he excavated many barrows in the locality and his findings were detailed and illustrated in his copious diaries. He recruited local miners to help him sink trial pits which they could do very quickly. His manuscripts remain an important resource in the study of the antiquities of the county. A number of artefacts uncovered by Skinner also survive in museum collections. He left other manuscripts and published accounts of a *West Country Tour* (1797), *Hadrian's Wall* (1801), and *The Isle of Anglesey* (1802).

Sadly Skinner was dogged by sudden deaths in the family. In 1810 his brother and two sisters died. In 1811 his youngest daughter died. In 1812 he lost his young wife Anna to consumption after only six years of marriage. He then had to bring up his remaining four children by himself. His favourite daughter Laura also died of consumption aged 14 in 1820, leaving him with his three sons. When he wasn't excavating barrows he was prone to depressions and he was increasingly ostracised by the local community; they thought him mad and towards the end even tied tin cans to the tails of his dogs. He was obviously a highly intelligent man and not cut out for the rough and tumble of a Somerset coal mining village that was going through social upheaval. He often found himself struggling to cope with the hardships of the poor and the unsympathetic attitudes of the wealthy landowners. Skinner tried to escape into antiquarian thought. For him Camerton was the *Camulodunum* of Tacitus, where Arthur had fought the traitor Mordred. Sometimes he would ride over to Stourhead to dine with Sir Richard Hoare, craving intelligent company. In the end his faith in humanity left him. Even his own sons turned against him and in his loneliness and depression in October 1839 he went off to a beech wood one day behind the rectory and committed suicide by shooting himself.

Skinner left 146 volumes of journals to the British Museum. A further twenty-five volumes of Skinner's papers were discovered in 1933 in a London bookseller's and in 1971 *The Journal of a Somerset Rector* was published in an enlarged edition covering the years 1803 to 1834.

Interestingly, Virginia Woolf wrote an account called *Life Itself* in 1927 which she expanded into *Two Parsons* in 1932, in which she contrasted Parson Woodforde, who liked his food and Mr Skinner who liked excavating his barrows. She too ended up committing suicide.

Rev Sydney Smith 1771-1845

ESSAYIST, REFORMER AND LIVELY WIT / Lived in Combe Florey 1829-45

Born in Woodford, Essex, Sydney Smith had French Protestant blood racing through his veins which he reckoned accounted for his lively nature. He was eminent, eccentric and Canon of St Paul's. In 1802 he helped found *The Edinburgh Review* and became its first editor, contributing articles for over 25 years. He also gave lectures in Moral Philosophy in London which were eventually published by his wife. In 1828 he moved down from Yorkshire to Combe Florey. On the death of his brother he inherited a mere £50,000, which put him 'out of the reach of poverty'.

About the rectory at Combe Florey he wrote "*This is a*

AUTHOR OF "PLYMLEY'S LETTERS ON THE CATHOLICS"

beautiful place… with a wood of three or four acres belonging to it close to the house, and a glebe of sixty acres surrounding it, in a country everywhere most beautiful and fertile'.

To Lady Grey, another old friend he wrote:

"My neighbours look very much like other people's neighbours; their remarks are generally of a meteorological nature."

Sydney Smith was always one for a quote or a quip; many are now memorable…

"Marriage resembles a pair of shears, so joined that they cannot be separated; often moving in opposite directions, yet always punishing anyone who comes between them."

"There is one piece of advice, in a life of study, which I think no one will object to; and that is, every now and then to be completely idle – to do nothing at all."

"As the French say, there are three sexes - men, women, and clergymen."

He referred to the Church as a branch of the civil service.

"Correspondences are like small-clothes before the invention of suspenders; it is impossible to keep them up."

"Poverty is no disgrace to a man, but it is confoundedly inconvenient."

"My idea of heaven is eating pâté de foie gras to the sound of trumpets."

"Whatever you are by nature, keep to it; never desert your line of talent. Be what nature intended you for and you will succeed."

One of his more endearing tricks to impress visitors was to put donkeys fitted with deer antlers into his crowds numbered 20,000 or more. It was the first time that England had seen such a mass movement take to the urban streets. Riot was feared by the authorities, particularly after the Luddite machine-breaking episodes of 1812, but most assemblies were peaceful. Henry Hunt was given the title 'Orator' by none other than William Cobbett. What Hunt wanted was universal male suffrage, annual general elections and a secret ballot. Not much to ask for…

When Hunt went to Manchester on 16th August 1819 he was due to speak in St Peter's Fields. The crowd, though peaceful, numbered 60-80,000. They knew trouble was brewing from the authorities and while Henry Hunt was starting to speak, the Manchester and Salford Yeomanry, the Cheshire Yeomanry and the 15th Hussars were brought in to disperse the crowd. They drew their sabres and charged. The crowd was held in place or 'kettled' by the 88th Infantry regiment with fixed bayonets. At least eleven people were killed by sabre cuts, and over 500 people, including many women, wounded or trampled under foot. This soon became known as the 'Peterloo' Massacre. Henry Hunt was arrested, tried and sentenced to two and a half years in prison, which he served in the infamous Ilchester Jail.

Here he not only wrote a three-volume auto-biography but also wrote, collated and published the findings of an enquiry into the prison conditions and the daily ignominies doled out by its sadistic gaoler William Bridle. Torture, bribery and licentious conduct were the order of the day, as well as bad food, and the pilfering of public accounts, not to mention the way in which executions were carried out, with men dangling over the river. There was an enquiry, much public indignation, and the Governor sacked, but Ilchester jail was not pulled down till 1843. Very little exists today of the Jail, apart from a few cottages near the bridge on the east bank of the river Yeo.

Many of Henry Hunt's radical views were, however, taken up by the Chartist Movement which eventually led to parliamentary reform and much later, Universal suffrage. Votes for women came much later.

George Mitchell
1827–1901

STONEMASON AND SOCIAL ACTIVIST / *Montacute born and Montacute bred*

Mitchell's memories of social deprivation in Montacute in the 1830s and 1840s are well worth reading. These were published in a slim volume in 1874 called *The Skeleton at the Plough or the Poor Farm Labourers of the West with the Autobiography and Reminiscences of George Mitchell* and were edited by Stephen Price of Wellington. George Mitchell started work on a farm aged five. He was 'dragged up pretty hard'.

"Our food consisted principally of little barley cake, potatoes and salt, tea kettle broth and barley flippet. Tea kettle broth consisted of a few pieces of bread soaked in hot water with a little salt, sometimes with a leek chopped up in it. Sometimes

I would pull a turnip in the fields and gnaw on it to prevent hunger gnawing at me."

When the potato famine of 1845 struck Somerset it was almost as bad as in parts of Ireland.

"The potato famine was a sad visitation on Montacute. The people had hitherto been as dependant on potatoes as were the Irish themselves, and the poor of the village suffered bitterly without a helping hand being extended to them. No money was collected for their relief. I believe one nobleman

gave the poor his advice at the time, which was to use curry powder."

It was in that year that Mitchell, aged 19, left the land and went up onto Ham Hill to start work as a stonemason. Later he went to seek his fortune in London, became a marble mason, and eventually set up his own business, living at 166 Brompton Road. What is interesting is that he was always conscious of the poor working conditions and pay of his fellow workers back in Somerset.

Demonstration, Ham Hill, Yeovil, Whit-Monday, 1877. Platform men numbered, include : (1) Joseph Arch ; (2) George Mitchell ; (8) Rev. W. Jubb ; (9) Winter, a Somerset leader ; (11) T. Halliday, miners' leader.

Mary Scott 1751-1793

POET / Lived in Milborne Port and Ilminster

Mary Scott was the mother of John Edward Taylor. Her family were originally from South Petherton but she lived in Milborne Port. Her father was a linen draper. In 1774 she produced *The Female Advocate*, a poem of 522 lines in rhyming couplets praising many women poets including some of her contemporaries: Sarah Fielding, sister to Henry Fielding, Helen Maria Williams, Catherine Macaulay, Lady Mary Chudleigh and Ann Laetitia Barbauld. Her writing was inspired by John Duncombe's *The Feminead* published in 1754 in praise of the accomplishments of women writers, and poets in particular. Mary Scott also started up a correspondence with Anna Steel and Anna Seward. She spent much of her time as a semi-invalid looking after her own elderly mother. In 1788, after a courtship which lasted over a decade, she married John Edward Taylor, and moved to Ilminster where her son, John Edward Taylor, was born. He later ran the *Manchester Guardian*. Mary Scott died in her third pregnancy, in 1793, at the age of forty-one.

Charles Prestwich Scott - C.P. Scott 1846-1932

EDITOR OF THE MANCHESTER GUARDIAN / Born in Bath

C.P. Scott's father Russell Scott was a partner in a coal company and his mother the daughter of a wine merchant. He went to Oxford and took up rowing and debating. As John Edward Taylor's nephew he was appointed editor of The *Manchester Guardian* in 1872 when he was only twenty-five, a post that he held for 57 years. He also owned the paper from 1907-1932. Over the years CP Scott took up the cudgels against poverty, social injustice and rampant imperialism. He wrote against Cecil Rhodes and his exploitation of Africa, as well as being opposed to the Boer War. In 1895, whilst still editor of the *Manchester Guardian*, he entered Parliament for Lancashire as a Liberal, remaining there for 10 years. During the early years of the First World War he campaigned against conscription, and in 1916 did not support the way in which the Easter Rising in Dublin was put down. He was in favour of female suffrage. It was CP Scott who introduced the Zionist chemist Chaim Weizmann to Lloyd George. Scott raised the quality of the paper's journalism until it became a liberal rival to *The Times*.

Scott's quotes, like Walter Bagehot's, are now legendary. 'A newspaper's primary office is the gathering of news. At the peril of its soul it must see that the supply is not tainted.' 'Television? The word is half Latin and half Greek. No good can come of it.' 'Truth like everything should be economized.' 'Comment is free, but facts are sacred.'

One his sons managed the newspaper, another Edward Taylor Scott, became editor. His grandson Laurence Prestwich Scott was the last member of the family to edit the paper. *The Guardian* is now owned by the Scott Trust.

Sir Isaac Pitman 1813-1897

INVENTOR OF PITMAN'S SHORTHAND / Lived in Bath for 58 years

Although not strictly a hack, his contribution to journalism has been incalculable. Pitman was born in

Trowbridge, Wiltshire. At first he became a weaver like his father and then a teacher in Wooton-under-Edge. He was always keen to use educational aids, even using a flute to help pupils sing multiplication tables. Isaac was an impatient man who wanted to speed up the process of writing longhand so he taught himself what he could from earlier works on stenography by William Harding and Samuel Taylor. By 1837 he had devised his own version called *Stenographic Sound-Hand*, which is now known as Pitman's Shorthand.

Isaac moved to Bath with his wife in 1839 and lived there for the next 58 years. Interestingly Pitman used his shorthand for conducting a secret affair with a young woman called Martha Watts who was living in their house... After a year or two, Mrs Pitman became suspicious and had some of his notes transcribed by his students.

Pitman produced twenty editions of his shorthand and even coined a new word, *phonography*. By 1874 Pitman had become a printer and publisher with works near the centre of Bath. He lived first in Nelson Place and then at 17 Royal Crescent.

To see: There is a memorial plaque on the north wall of Bath Abbey.

Walter Bagehot 1826-1877

ECONOMIST, JOURNALIST AND WIT / Born and died in Langport

Walter Bagehot was the son of a banker. His mother was Edith Stuckey of Stuckey's Bank in Langport, so he had economics on both sides of the family. He was educated at Langport Grammar School, Bristol College and University College, London. He took a first-class degree in classics in 1846 and then stayed on to study political economy, metaphysics, and philosophy, earning the MA degree and a gold medal in philosophy. He witnessed the *coup d'etat* in Paris of Louis Napoleon in 1851 and was called to the Bar in 1852. Bagehot then worked at the family bank in Langport, then in Bristol, With a more than usual literary bent, he helped the *National Review* and was its co-editor and contributed twenty-nine articles, including 'The first

Edinburgh reviewers', 'Parliamentary reform', and pieces on Shakespeare, Cowper, Shelley, Dickens, Gibbon, Scott, Macaulay, and Peel. In 1858 he very wisely married Elizabeth Wilson, whose father just happened to be the editor of the *Economist*. Bagehot then moved to Clevedon. In 1860 Bagehot succeeded his father-in-law, James Wilson as editor of the *Economist* until his own death in 1877.

Bagehot was the author of *The English Constitution* in 1867, a work still widely read today. His interpretation of the role of Monarchy was even studied by George V.

Bagehot also wrote many articles about the American Civil War. *Lombard Street* was published in 1873. He coined the phrase 'boom and bust' and realised that economies worked in cycles. Maybe he had been reading Malthus, who had his own theory of *gluts* (see page 39). Bagehot favoured free trade and competition, criticized protection and monopoly. Interestingly he also had his doubts about imperial expansion. He often advocated *laissez-faire* policies, supported income tax, favoured nationalization of the railways, and approved proposals for a universal coinage and decimalization. Many of his arguments still hold water today. 'In crisis it is better to do nothing than to apply half measures.' Bagehot invented the Treasury bill and Gladstone referred to him as 'a sort of supplementary Chancellor of the Exchequer'. He was in effect one of the most influential people on Victorian economic policy. His works have been translated in many languages. He died of pneumonia at Hurds Hill, Langport, aged only 51.

To see: Walter Bagehot's grave in Langport churchyard has a wonderful view overlooking the River Parrett and West Moor towards Burrow Hill and Ham Hill. The editor of the *Economist* still lays a wreath every year.

Sir Arthur Pearson 1866–1921

FOUNDER OF THE DAILY EXPRESS / Born in Wookey

Cyril Arthur Pearson was the son of the vicar of Wookey who later moved to a parish in Buckinghamshire. In the 1880s Arthur became a journalist in London, worked for George Newnes. After six years he left to found his own periodical called *Pearson's Weekly*; it sold 250,000 copies in its first issue. Arthur went from strength to strength,

always managing to set up various charities where they were needed, including the Fresh Air Fund to enable disadvantaged children to take part in outdoor holidays and adventures.

In 1898 he purchased the *Morning Herald* and in 1900 merged it into the *Daily Express* which was sold for 1/2d, in contrast to Harmsworth's 1d *Daily Mail*. It carried news on the front page instead of advertisements. In 1904 he purchased the struggling *Standard* and its sister paper the *Evening Standard* for £700,000. His empire

grew and grew but Arthur Pearson began to lose his sight. By 1910 he had to give up work on the *Express*. Eventually it passed to Max Aitken.

In 1915, Pearson founded St Dunstan's Home a charity for soldiers who had been blinded by gas or shellfire during the First World War. He encouraged them to take up handicrafts such as basket making. (St Dunstan's now has a large centre at Ovingdean near Brighton.) Pearson was also a close friend of Baden Powell and they managed to get *The Scout* magazine printed in Braille.

Pearson died in December 1921 when he slipped in his bath and hit his head and drowned. He is buried in Hampstead.

Lord Beaverbrook – Max Aitken 1879-1964

NEWSPAPER TYCOON / Owned Cricket Court at Cricket Malherbie, Stowey Court at Nether Stowey and many farms in Somerset

Born in Canada, Max Aitken made his way to England before the First World War. He purchased The *Daily Express* in 1916 and in 1918 he founded the *Sunday Express*. He also owned the *London Evening Standard*. In 1916 his book *Canada in Flanders* was published, documenting the achievements of Canadians fighting on the Western Front. After the War, he wrote several books including *Politicians and the Press* and *Politicians and the War*. At one time Beaverbrook employed Evelyn Waugh as a journalist. Waugh later used Beaverbrook as a model for two of his characters, Lord Copper in *Scoop* and as Lord Monomark in *Put Out More Flags* and *Vile Bodies*.

During the Second World War, Beaverbrook was close friends with Winston Churchill, who appointed him Minister for Aircraft Production and then Minister of Supply. At the same time Beaverbrook expanded his farming empire from Manor Farm, Cricket Malherbie, buying Stowey Court at Nether Stowey as well a string of other run-down farms. He built up his butter and cheese empire which is still based in Nether Stowey called Cricketer Farms. Lord Beaverbrook also made friends with the other Mr Churchill, Bill Churchill, the famous blacksmith and cider-maker in Dowlish Wake.

When visiting Somerset, Beaverbrook often stayed at Cricket Court, a fine house which he had bought. It was built in 1811 for the second Earl of Chatham, William Pitt the elder's eldest son. After Beaverbrook, Cricket Court was owned for a while by the historian Count Tolstoy. It has a wonderful circular library. To the west side of the house is a circular sunken garden which had been used as a medieval bear pit. I once sheared Jacob sheep there for Harry Hook who owned the house at the time. The bears had long since disappeared.

Lord Rees-Mogg 1928-

JOURNALIST AND EDITOR / Born in Bristol · Lives near Mells

William Rees-Mogg went to Oxford and in 1952 began to work for *The Financial Times*. In 1960 he moved to *The Sunday Times* and became its deputy editor. He then became editor of *The Times* from 1967 to 1981. He was Vice-Chairman of the Board of Governors of the BBC and chairman of the Arts Council. He was High Sheriff of Somerset from 1978 to 1979 and was made a life peer in 1988 as Baron Rees-Mogg of Hinton Blewitt. Since 1992 he has been a regular columnist for *The Times* and *The Mail on Sunday* since 2004, writing on a variety of contemporary issues. He has also found time to write several books, including *How to Buy Rare Books* (1985) *The Great Reckoning* (1993) and *The Sovereign Individual* (1999). Rees-Mogg's family have owned land on Mendip for generations.

Christopher Booker 1937-

JOURNALIST / Lives near Chewton Mendip

Christopher Booker grew up near Ilminster, in the house owned by the family of John Hanning Speke (see page 142). In 1959 Christopher Booker became a jazz critic for the *Daily Telegraph* and *Sunday Telegraph*, then a political scriptwriter for *That Was The Week That Was*. In 1961 he helped found one of this country's leading satirical magazines with Richard Ingrams and Willie Rushton. He was *Private Eye's* first editor and has been a member of their writing team ever since. He is also a very long-serving columnist in both the *Spectator* and *Sunday Telegraph*.

Blaydon Compton ChedderRock Hemington Lauerton
Luxton Stone Afton Midfumer Norton Hardington Beckington
Paſſage Bidcham Chilcompton Kilmerfden Orcherley
impſham Axbridge Chedder Mineries Chewton Mendip KILMERSDEN Buckland Brackley
RokesBridge Badſworth Mendip Hills Enborough Straton in the Vorſwey Babbington Elm Walles
rough BRENT Chedder Priddy HVND Mells
EaſtBrent HVND Radneſtocke WELLS Banager Holcombe FromeSellwood
WeſtBrent Allerton Aſhwick Ligh Vader Mendip Whateley HVND
inham BEMPSTONE Eaſt Marck Wedmore HUND Cole Pitts Stoke Land Nannye de la Mare Merſton Bigot Cast Selwood
HighBridge Ochy of Wokey Hole Westbury WELLS Dunnyet Witham Clauford
R Crent marſh HVND Gedney more al or Theodorodunum Paulting EaſtCronmere Charterhouſe
Baſtian THE BELGE Moor Poor Godeney Hudel Croſcomb Westranmer Fryere Foreſt
Brent Bridge Wike Shepton Wanſtrow
Marſh BurtleHouſe Gedney Taſham Malley Segemore WHIS: Cheſter Black WeſtComb BRUTON
Wollavington Heath moor Meare HartlackBridge N.Wotton Cumpton Dundo Euerick at Veſton noble Killman
WHITELEGH Shapwick Avalon or Areland Isle Pilton Euerſhurch Batcomb Burcomlodge
Cuſſington Sharpham Park GLASTON TON Pull Euerich Park Milton Bruham Longleat
Chilton Edington Aſhton Glaſenbury the Tower HVND WestPenard EaſtPenard Hichiat HVND
Stoke HVND Walton Street HVND Bridley Stone Chappel Lamyat Bruton
Sutton Morlinch Greinton Irythorne SouthWalton Hornblotton Almiſford Wick Staffordell
Weſton Sedge moor Butley WestLidford Eaſt Alford Apitcomb Ridlinch Knolle NORTON Pen
Queenſmore Middleſoy Audre moor CumptonDundo Barton Balborquak Lovington Caſtle Caree Shepton Mountague Burton FERRIS Stoke Cucklington
N.More Andre KineWeston Wheathill Charlton mujowaue Winec aunton Pen HUND
Athelney Michaelsborough Higham WestCharlton Kyneton NorthBarrow Yarlington Halton
Anthony Longham EaſtCharlton CATTESASH Cadbury Buckhorn West.
SOMERTON Lites Care Bitcarge So Barrow HVND Blackford Maperton Cheriton
Auler Somerton Haſtingroue Sutton Sparkford Compton Paunford Horſington Kyneton
Langport Pitney HVND Milton WestCarnel Sutton Weſton Cadbury Witcomb Comeleck Stour Weſtou
Gregorytake Hewiſh PITNEY Kingſdon Hulton North Oſſen Quincamell Günvl Charltoncast HORE
Curryreuell LongSutton Barwick Brode Kington Stowell Abbas Comb Temple Comb
Swill Ordred R Ilcheſter in Chilton Adber Corton Week Venston
BULSTONE FifeHead Muckenay PillBridge Tintinull HUND Aſhunton Samford Dorcas Pountington Tulmner
Illbruers Thornaybridge Longlode HUND Multford HORNE HUND Milburne port Henstridg
Abbot Leigh Kingſbury MARTOCK Witcomb Aſh Trent Oburde Cakdlepurſe Stalbridge
Crockham Pokinton Lambrock Martock Tintinhul Wether Compton Gothull
Illon Barrington STONE Yeouil or Evill
Stocklinch S PETHER Shepton Beauchamp Chiltern Dumer UpperCompto Haydon
Magdalen TON SouthPetherton Thorpe HVND Glaſenbradford
Stocklinch Otterſey Seuington Stoke Montecute Luſton Berwick Thornford
Whitlackington SeuingtonMaries Tintinhull HUND Brunp Ham Tillington
HVND ter Hamden

16 HARDY IN YEOVIL

Thomas Hardy 1840-1928

NOVELIST / Lived in Yeovil 1876

It may come as a surprise to some people, but Thomas Hardy, the famous Dorset novelist, lived in Somerset, albeit briefly. In March 1876, with his new wife Emma in tow, Thomas moved from Swanage, where they had spent their honeymoon, to Yeovil, into temporary lodgings. They lived at 7 Peter Street, in the middle of town. The only furniture they possessed was a bookcase and a door scraper. Yeovil was not unknown to Hardy's family as his mother, Jemima Hand, when she was a young girl, lived only a few miles away in Melbury Osmond and she would often visit Yeovil on market day. Once she recalled seeing a child whipped at the cart-tail round Yeovil for stealing a book from a book-stall. In her new biography of Hardy, Claire Tomalin wonders if this child was not Hardy's mother herself, which would make Yeovil and books an interesting psychological combination, as if Hardy, by being a writer, was atoning for his mother's crime, or at least fulfilling her wishes to become better acquainted with literature.

When Thomas Hardy came to Yeovil, he was 35. In April 1876 his fifth novel, *The Hand of Ethelberta*, was published in London. At the end of May 1876 the young couple left for a tour of Holland and the Rhine land. Hardy visited the site of the battle of Waterloo and upon his return talked to the last of the old Chelsea pensioners who had fought in that battle. The Hardys returned to Yeovil in June, but in early July moved to Sturminster Newton where they lived beside the River Stour.

In Hardy's books Yeovil is known as "Ivell" which is

closer to its Saxon name of *Gifle* recorded in 880AD. (The word Gifl means 'forked river or confluence'. Other words for Yeovil are *Givele, Yeule and Euill*).

To Visit: Yeovil. Where 7 Peter Street once stood has now become a private car park for a shop which specialises in cheap knickers, blouses and skirts. The only blue plaque, however, says "Primark Private Parking."

One of Thomas Hardy's other connections with Somerset is with Dunster. In 1881 he set *The Laodicean* in Dunster with its famous castle. The hero is a young architect (ie Thomas Hardy himself) called George Somerset. Dunster is *Markton* with its own castle, *Stancy Castle*. The village of Carhampton is called *Sleeping Green* with a small inn which must be The Butcher's Arms. Lord Quantock Arms is the Luttrell Arms in Dunster. *The Laodicean*, although not as well known as his other Dorset books, is the most autobiographical of Hardy's novels and one of the most optimistic. (The term *Laodicean* means lukewarm, neither waxing hot nor cold about religion or politics.)

Hardy also wrote *Our Exploits at West Poley* in 1883, just before the *Mayor of Casterbridge*, it was originally serialised in the Boston magazine, *The Household*, between November 1892 and April 1893. It is a children's story, where a boy goes to stay with his widowed aunt and older boy cousin Steve in West Poley. The two boys become friends and explore the caves in the nearby Mendips where they find a secret cave inside a larger one with a subterranean stream.The lads create havoc when they divert a stream from one passage to another, resulting in West Poley losing a water supply and East Poley gaining one.

Other places mentioned by Hardy in Somerset include *The Windwhistle Inn*, set high up near Cricket St Thomas between Crewkerne and Chard, which is mentioned by name in *The Trampwoman's Tragedy*.

> *Lone inns we loved, my man and I,*
> *My man and I;*
> *'King's Stag', 'Windwhistle' high and dry,*
> *'The Horse' on Hintock Green,*
> *The cosy house at Wynyard's Gap,*
> *'The Hut', renowned on Bredy Knap,*
> *And many another wayside tap*
> *Where folk might sit unseen.*

HARDY'S SOMERSET PLAENARIES

Aquae Sulis	=	itself, being the Roman name for Bath, Avon.
Castle Inn	=	itself, 7 Middle Street, Yeovil, Somerset (demolished in the 1920s).
Falls Park	=	Mells Park, near Frome, Somerset.
Fountall	=	Wells, Somerset.
Glaston	=	itself, being Glastonbury, Somerset.
Ivel or Ivell	=	Yeovil, Somerset.
Ivelchester	=	Ilchester, Somerset.
Ivel Way	=	Long Ash Lane, now the A37 road from Dorchester to Yeovil.
Markton	=	Dunster, Somerset.
Marshall's Elm	=	itself, on the Polden Hills a mile south of Street, Somerset.
Narrobourne	=	West Coker, near Yeovil, Somerset.
Outer Wessex	=	Somerset.
Sleeping Green	=	village green in the area of Carhampton.
Stancy Castle	=	Dunster Castle, Dunster, Somerset.
Toneborough	=	Taunton, Somerset (which is on the River Tone).
Deane	=	Vale of Taunton Deane, Somerset.
Wyll's Neck	=	in the Quantock Hills, Somerset.

17 MONTACUTE AND THE POWYS CLAN

THE LARGE, GARRULOUS and gifted Powys family came to Montacute in 1885. Their father, Charles Powys, was its vicar and had the living for 32 years until 1918. Charles was born at Stalbridge and had been curate in Dorchester in order to be near his mother in Weymouth. His wife Mary was descended from the poet and hymn writer William Cowper 1731–1800. There were eleven children. All were artistic and three of the boys, John, Theodore and Llewellyn became full-time writers. Of the girls, Gertrude was a painter who studied at the Slade and in Paris, Nellie died of appendicitis aged only 13, Philippa, was a poet who worked on Abbey farm, Marian went to New York and became an authority on lace, Lucy became a recluse. Of the other boys, Littleton became headmaster of Sherborne preparatory school, William a farmer in Kenya and Albert an architect who worked for S.P.A.B. (The Society for Protection of Ancient Buildings founded in 1877 by Ruskin and Morris). Albert helped save Montacute House as it was about to be demolished in the 1930s, by suggesting that the National Trust bought it, which they did. Thomas Hardy used to visit the Powys family when he was in the area. Not surprisingly there is an active Powys Society.

John Cowper Powys, 1872–1963

WRITER, LECTURER AND PHILOSOPHER / Lived in Montacute

John Cowper Powys was 13 when his family moved to Montacute. In the 1891 census he is registered as still living at Montacute, aged 18, a student at Sherborne. He went to Cambridge, read history and became a peripatetic teacher of English, lecturing at various girls' schools and moved to the States. He first published *Odes and Other Poems* in 1896. More poems followed and then his first novel *Wood and Stone* and a second, *Rodmoor*. He also produced three books of literary criticism as well as *Confessions of Two Brothers* with his brother Llewelyn. He then moved back to the States and got into his stride. Between 1925-28 he wrote *Wolf Solent*, an earthy intense, almost Dostoyevskian novel set in the countryside around *Ramsgard* and *Blacksod* (Sherborne and Yeovil). Its characters include the young teacher, Wolf Solent, caught between the caresses of Gerda Torp, the stone cutter's beautiful daughter and Christie, the well-read daughter of Mr Malakite the bookseller. Then there are Otter Weevil and Bess Round and places such as Lenty Pond and Dead Badger Lane; even the Kingsbury (Episcopi) band is mentioned.

Gerda is a sparkling beauty, a charming wild flower whose 'beauty was so startling that it seemed to destroy in a moment all ordinary human relations'. She gives herself to Wolf in an 'empty cow-barn, its roof thatched with river-reeds and its floor thickly strewn with a clean, dry bed of last autumn's yellow bracken.'

Wolf Solent was followed by *A Glastonbury Romance* (1932) which looks at contemporary Glastonbury and the legends of the Holy Grail. This cost Powys dearly in an out-of-court settlement with a Glastonbury dignitary who thought he had been portrayed in the book. He returned to Britain in 1934; wrote *Weymouth Sands* and *Maiden Castle*. The landscapes and places are as important to his novels as his characters. Cowper Powys's novels were much admired in Hungary.

Powys also wrote a whole string of books on philosophy as well as an autobiography. He retired to Wales but after his death his ashes were scattered on Chesil Beach, in Dorset.

Many people have drawn inspiration from his long rambling novels which create a world of their own. "Powys evoked the English landscape with an almost sexual intensity. Hardy comes to mind, but a Hardy drunk and feverish with mystical exuberance." - Philip Pullman.

Margaret Drabble recently wrote an article in the *Guardian* on John Cowper entitled *The English Degenerate*, 'He is dangerous and the reader may wander for years in this parallel universe.'

Theodore Powys 1875-1953

NOVELIST / Lived in Montacute

Theodore moved to Montacute when he was ten. Unlike his elder brother John, he was sent to school in Suffolk and was deeply religious. For a short while he became a farmer and then lived the life of a hermit in Studland and Chaldon Herring near the Dorset Coast. Eventually he went inland to Mappowder. In 1905 he married Violet, the eighteen-year-old daughter of the local solicitor. His works include *The Soliloquy of a Hermit*, *Black Bryony*, *Mr. Weston's Good Wine*, *Kindness in a Corner*, *Mark Only*. *Unclay*, *Rosie Plum* and *Father Adam* were published posthumously. He is buried at Mappowder.

Llewelyn Powys 1884–1939

NOVELIST AND ESSAYIST / Lived in Montacute

Llewelyn Powys moved to Montacute when he was only one, so of all the Powys brothers, Montacute left the deepest impression on him, and this is borne out in his writing. He worked on the land at Batemore on top of

Ham Hill near Odcombe and then went to Cambridge. Later, despite contracting TB, he travelled to America, Switzerland and Africa. His many fictional works include *Apples be Ripe*, *Ebony and Ivory* and *Black Laughter*. In the last two years of his life he wrote some fine essays about Somerset and Dorset with vivid descriptions of Montacute, Exmoor, Ilchester Gaol, The River Yeo, Rosamund Clifford and Ham Hill. See *Somerset Essays*, *Rats in the Sacristy*, *The Book of Days* and *A Baker's Dozen*. He died near Davos. After the war, his ashes were brought back and buried on the cliff-top near East Chaldon in Dorset.

"Llewelyn Powys is one of those rare writers who teach endurance of life as well as its enjoyment." – Philip Larkin.

Phillipa Powys 1886–1963

NOVELIST AND POET / Born in Montacute

Phillipa, otherwise known as Katie, grew up in the shadow of her elder brothers. She had no formal education apart from what her governess taught her and so she worked on the neighbouring Abbey Farm. She loved cattle, cheese and butter making. Apparently she used to smoke a pipe and wore heavy labourer's boots. She spent most of her life farming in the Montacute area but in 1924 moved to the Dorset coast, to a cottage called Chydyok near East Chaldon. Her brothers Llewellyn and Theodore lived nearby. She wrote several novels but only one of them was ever published: *The Blackthorn Winter*. Other novels were called *The Tragedy of Budvale*, *Joan Callais* and a play called *The Quick and the Dead*. Her poems were published under the title of *Driftwood*. She also kept a journal and had a secret lover, a fisherman from Lulworth Cove, one of the Miller clan whom she met on the clifftops. After his death she moved inland to Buckland Newton.

Herbert by his great-granddaughter Margaret Fitzherbert and published by John Murray in 1983.

To see: The recumbent effigy of Colonel Aubrey Herbert, his sword hanging over the tomb in the Lutyens Chapel, in Brushford Church just over the River Barle and south of Dulverton.

Evelyn Waugh 1903-1966

NOVELIST AND NOTED WIT / Lived in Combe Florey

Evelyn was the second son of Arthur Waugh and younger brother of Alec Waugh. He was born in Hampstead and his first ventures into literature were in 1912, writing and editing a small magazine for his children's gang called the Pistol Troop. As a young boy he would go and stay with his maiden aunts in Midsomer Norton which he rather liked: "I suppose that in fact I never spent longer than two months there in any year, but the place captivated my imagination as my true home never did".

In 1917 his brother Alec's first venture into writing caused more of a stir, when *The Loom of Youth* was published. It tackled the taboo subject of homosexuality in boys' public schools, in his case Sherborne. So to avoid any repeat embarrassment at Sherborne, Evelyn was sent to Lancing and to Oxford where he fell in with the 'Brideshead Revisited' set. He became a prep-school teacher and the various schools he taught at became models for his first novel, *Decline and Fall*. It was soon followed by *Vile Bodies*, *Black Mischief* (about the Ethiopian Emperor, Haile Selassie), *A Handful of Dust*, *Scoop* (featuring war reporters in Abyssinia) and *Put Out More Flags* a satire on the ludicrous nature of the phoney war.

During the Second World War Evelyn Waugh joined the commandos. He took part in an abortive attempt to take Dakar, held by the Vichy French and also in raids on Libya and the evacuation of Crete. In 1944 he went on a quasi-diplomatic mission to Yugoslavia with Randolph Churchill, narrowly escaping capture when German gliders and paratroops made a surprise attack on the partisans' headquarters where they were staying. Good training for Somerset.

After the war came *Brideshead Revisited*, *The Loved One* and the trilogy *Sword of Honour*. Evelyn Waugh moved to Combe Florey in 1956. To avoid being pestered he had a sign carved in stone at the entrance which says simply "No Admittance on Business".

When Evelyn died in 1966 his will stated that his royalties should be left to his offspring in an account called the 'Save the Children Fund'. He is buried at Combe Florey.

To see: Evelyn Waugh's grave is at the back of the churchyard in Combe Florey and can be approached through a small gate. Evelyn is buried next to his second wife Laura Herbert, daughter of Aubrey Herbert.

Auberon Waugh 1939-2001

NOVELIST, JOURNALIST AND CRITIC / Born at Pixton Park, Dulverton

The Waugh family moved to Combe Florey when Auberon was seventeen. Known as 'Bron', he did his National Service in Cyprus where he rather foolishly grabbed a machine gun mounted on his armoured car by its muzzle, and because it had jammed, he shook it. Six rounds went through him at point blank range. He was lucky to survive, he recovered and went to Oxford to read PPE.

too attractive to otherwise nice and sensible women.' Auberon moved back to Combe Florey when his mother died. His wife Lady Teresa Waugh is a translator and novelist. Her books include *Painting Water*, *Waterloo Waterloo*, *Intolerable Burden*, *Song at Twilight*, *Sylvia's Lot*, *The Entertaining Book*, *The Gossips* and *The House*. All their children Alexander, Nathaniel, Sophia and Daisy have become writers in their own way. Auberon died at Combe Florey and is buried there.

To see: Auberon's grave is in the new plot on the opposite side of the road from Combe Florey church.

Alexander Waugh 1963-

Author and journalist / Lives near Milverton

Son of Auberon Waugh, Alexander Waugh is very definitely a chip off the old block. He read music at Manchester and worked there as an impresario and concert agent. He was Opera Critic of the *Mail on Sunday* and the *Evening Standard*. He reviews books for many national newspapers and is also a cartoonist. In 1995 he wrote *Classical Music, A New Way of Listening* which has been translated into fourteen foreign languages. His other books are *Time and God* as well as a perceptive insight into his own literary family called *Fathers and Sons* which was turned into a documentary film for BBC Four. His latest book, *The House of Wittgenstein*, was published in England in 2008. He has a good website which contains amongst other things a long list of his father's humorous or irascible quotations.

Auberon Waugh wrote five novels: *The Foxglove Saga* (1960) *Path of Dalliance* (1963) *Who Are The Violets Now?* (1965) *Consider the Lilies* (1968) *A Bed of Flowers* (1972). He is best known for his work as a journalist on many newspapers and magazines including *The Spectator*, *The New Statesman* and *Private Eye*. He did not review any poetry that did not rhyme. Indeed he did not like poets at all; they were banned from his Academy Club on the grounds that 'they did not pay for their drinks and were

PART THREE

FROM EXMOOR TO SEDGEMOOR

View of Minehead
Coast. Drawn by
J. M. W. Turner RA,
engraved by
W. B. Cooke

19 NOT JUST BRIGANDS AND DEER-STALKERS...

T HE FORREST OF EXMOORE: "a solitarie place, the more commodius for Stagges who keepe possession of it." THOMAS GERARD 1632

Exmoor, Brendons and Quantock: these are still wild, hard places to make a living. Stories hang around for hundreds of years and are then spun into a fine yarn.

R.D. Blackmore 1825-1900

NOVELIST AND AUTHOR OF LORNA DOONE

The family of Richard Doddridge Blackmore came from the Parracombe region of Exmoor. He was educated at King's School, Bruton and Blundells in Tiverton. After training as a lawyer at the Middle Temple he inherited money and set up as a market gardener in Teddington, Middlesex to supplement his writing. He produced fifteen novels and books of poems: *Poems by Melanter*, *Epullia*, *The Bugle of the Black Sea*, *Clara Vaughan* and *Craddock Nowell* which was set in the New Forest. In 1865 Blackmore and his wife Lucy went on holiday to Exmoor. It is from this trip that he gained much material for his next book, *Lorna Doone*. They stayed at several inns, including The Ship Inn at Porlock.

The tale of the Doones is said to been based on real events on Exmoor related to Blackmore by his uncle, who was rector of Oare church. It is set at the time of the Monmouth Rebellion in 1685 and charts the ups and downs of everyday Exmoor folk: the Doones and Ridds. It was in Oare church that Lorna Doone was shot by her half-brother Carver Doone as she stood at the altar to marry John Ridd.

Lorna Doone was first published anonymously in 1869, in a limited three-volume edition of just 500 copies, of which only 300 sold. It then took off with a cheaper single-volume edition.

To visit: Oare church where there is a memorial to R.D. Blackmore. Another memorial stone stands about a mile south of Malmsmead bridge in Badgworthy Valley, now known as Doone Valley. In Dulverton there is a statue of Lorna Doone outside the Exmoor National Park headquarters, which was once the local workhouse. There are countless Lorna Doone teashops…

Alice King 1839-1894

NOVELIST, WRITER AND MUSICIAN / Lived at Cutcombe near Wheddon Cross

Alice King's father was the vicar of Cutcombe, a remote parish on Exmoor near Wheddon Cross. The church is the highest on Exmoor. Alice was blind from early childhood, but wrote many novels and poems and was also a very gifted musician. She formed her own band, spoke several languages, and used to visit Italy regularly. She also had a favourite pony that she used to ride out on Exmoor. Her books include *Forest Keep*, *Spell Bound*, *Queen of Herself* and *A Cluster of Lives*.

She also wrote many magazine articles for *Argosy* and *The Smart Set* on any subject from Alexander Pope, Swift and Coleridge to Mary Wollstonecraft and Exmoor.

To see: Cutcombe Church.

Richard Jefferies 1848-1887

JOURNALIST, NOVELIST AND NATURE WRITER / Visited Exmoor 1882

Jefferies visited Exmoor in the summer of 1882 and wrote *Red Deer* in 1884 as a result, as well as an article called *Summer in Somerset* for the *English Illustrated Magazine*. Born at Coate on the outskirts of Swindon, Jefferies, as a young man, had access to the library of William Morris who lived nearby at Kelmscott. To supplement his living as a journalist on the *North Wilts Herald* Jefferies started writing novels and nature books. He was always dogged by illness and ulcers, probably from overwork, and in 1882, to get a bit of peace and quiet, he visited Exmoor. He stayed with his friend, the artist John William North who lived on the Brendons in various places such as Withycombe, Bilbrook and Leighland. The 1881 census shows North, staying at Bicknoller described as an artist in water colours. Jefferies' account of red deer is meticulously researched; he had interviewed various huntsmen including Arthur Heal of the Devon and Somerset Staghounds, who lived at North Ley and his son Fred who had several farms around Exford. (Arthur Heal was the maternal great grandfather of Arthur C Clarke see p158).

"The chase of the wild stag is a bit out of the life of the fifteenth century brought down to our own time."

"Suddenly, as I looked once more, I caught sight of a red mark in the midst of an acre of brake surrounded by oak. I was sure it was a stag instantly by the bright colour, by the position, and yet if questioned I could not have positively asserted that I had any reason for my opinion at all. Certainty does not always depend upon proofs that can be explained. A secret judgement exists in the mind and acts on perceptions too delicate to be registered. I was certain it was a stag, and the glass at once confirmed my eyes.

He was standing in the fern beside a bush, with his head down as if feeding. The great oak woods were about him, above and below, and the sunlight fell on the golden red of his coat. A whistle – the sound was a moment or two reaching him – made him lift his head, and the upright carriage of the neck proved again that it was a stag and not a hind. His antlers had not yet risen as high as his ears…He moved easily along the steep slope where even hounds sometimes find a difficulty in following. "

"There is no more beautiful creature than a stag in his pride of antler, his coat of ruddy gold, his grace of form and motion. He seems the natural owner of the ferny coombes, the oak woods, the broad slopes of heather. They belong to him, and he steps upon the sward in lordly mastership. The land is his, and the hills, the sweet streams and rocky glens. He is infinitely more natural than the cattle and sheep that have strayed into his domains. For some inexplicable reason, although they too are in reality natural, when he is present they look as if they had been put there and were kept there by artificial means. They do not, as painters say, shade in with the colours and shape of the landscape. He is as natural as an oak, or a fern, or a rock itself. He is earth–born – autochthon – and holds possession by descent. Utterly scorning control, the walls and hedges are nothing to him – he roams where he chooses, as fancy leads, and gathers the food that pleases him."   From *Red Deer*

I drifted like a leaf detached from a tree, across to a deep coombe in the Quantock Hills. The vast hollow is made for repose and lotus-eating; its very shape, like a hammock, indicates idleness. There the days go over noiselessly and without effort, like white summer clouds. Ridges each side rise high and heroically steep––it would be proper to set out and climb them, but not to-day, not now: some time presently. To the left massive Will's Neck stands out in black shadow defined and distinct, like a fragment of night in the bright light of the day. The wild red deer lie there, but the mountain is afar; a sigh is all I can give to it, for the Somerset sun is warm and the lotus sweet. Yonder, if the misty heat moves on, the dim line of Dunkery winds along the sky, not unlike the curved back of a crouching hare.

From *Summer in Somerset*

In all Jefferies wrote 22 books including *Amaryllis at the Fair*, *The Story of My Heart*, *Bevis: the story of a boy*, *The Amateur Poacher* and *The Gamekeeper at Home*. Richard Jefferies died when he was only 38.

Sir Francis Carruthers Gould 1844–1925

POLITICAL CARTOONIST AND AUTHOR / Lived in Porlock

Born in Barnstaple, Gould went to London and worked on the *Pall Mall Gazette* and the *Westminster Gazette*. He also wrote and illustrated his own books: *Who killed Cock Robin?*, *Tales told in the Zoo*, two volumes of *Froissart's Modern Chronicles*, and *Picture Politics*. He was knighted in 1906, the first political cartoonist to be so honoured. He retired to Porlock in 1914 and lived there for eleven years until his death in 1925. In his spare time he worked on a delightful book called *Nature Caricatures, Sketches from Exmoor* which was published in 1929. His work was often signed simply FCG.

Berta Lawrence 1906–2003

NOVELIST, WRITER AND POET / Lived in Wembdon, near Bridgwater

Berta was born in Buckinghamshire but moved to Wembdon in 1932 with her husband Jack Lawrence, whom she had met whilst teaching in France. Jack taught for many years at Dr Morgan's school in Bridgwater, while Berta taught French at the Girls' Grammar School and English at the French convent in Langport. She would go there by bus, often through the floods in winter. Berta wrote eight books which included two novels: *The Bond of Green Withy* about the Somerset Levels between the wars set around Stoke St Gregory, while *The Nightingale in the Branches* is set on a Quantock farm. She wrote many excellent guides such as *Quantock Country*, *Wordsworth and Coleridge in Somerset* and essays about the Brendons and Exmoor.

She also wrote many poems and contributed articles to the *Guardian*, the *Countryman* and the *Western Morning News*. Her *Somerset Journal* contains an excellent essay on Walter Raymond. She also wrote many children's stories which were broadcast by the BBC on *Children's Hour* in the 1940s. Some of her best poems appeared in the *Exmoor Review*. Her husband Jack Lawrence wrote *Men and Mining in the Quantocks*. Much of his research into the medieval history of Bridgwater was incorporated into the *Victoria County History of Somerset* and a book on Bridgwater written by Dr Robert Dunning.

A History of Bridgwater by Jack Lawrence has recently been revised and completed by his son, J.C. Lawrence.

Ernest William Hendy 1873–1950

POET AND ORNITHOLOGIST / Lived in Porlock 1923–1950

Born in Trowbridge, Hendy went to school in Devon and read law at Oxford. He was a solicitor in Manchester for most of his working life and retired to West Somerset in 1923. A keen naturalist, this is reflected in his writing. He was very much concerned with bird protection, and wrote a number of books about birds and Exmoor, focussing particularly upon bird migration. His books which are very collectable included a book of verse called *Selworthy and other poems*, *Wild Exmoor through the Year*, *Somerset Birds and Some Other Folk*, *Here and There with Birds* and *More about Birds*.

To see: There is a memorial tablet to Hendy in the church at Luccombe.

Victor Bonham Carter 1913-2007

Author and publisher / *Lived at Brushford, East Anstey and Milverton*

Victor Bonham Carter was born in Maidstone. After reading Modern Languages at Cambridge, he had a variety of jobs including being a schoolmaster and sub-editor of the *Countryman*. He wrote many articles for them and the *Illustrated London News*. He was very interested in fine art, music and farming and at one stage even considered a career as a concert pianist. After the Second World War he went back to the land, first in Berkshire and then in 1947 at Langaller Farm, Brushford, near Dulverton. He became associated with the Elmhirsts and co-authored a book on Dartington Hall as well as researching the rural Arts and Crafts movement. He moved to East Anstey in 1956. He also worked for the BBC Home service in Bristol, writing scripts and presenting pro-grammes. Bonham Carter also wrote books on rural matters: *The English Village, Farming the Land, Exploring Parish Churches, The Survival of the English Countryside*. In 1976 he left East Anstey and a few years later moved to Milverton where he stayed for the rest of his life.

In 1964 Victor became Chairman of the Exmoor Society and five years later in partnership with Tim Burton he set up a publishing company called Exmoor Press. For thirty years he was also editor or co-editor of the Exmoor Society's magazine, *The Exmoor Review*. He also worked very closely with the Authors' Society and would always champion the rights of authors. He also wrote other books: *The Essence of Exmoor, Soldier True, Authors by Profession* and an autobiography *What Countryman Sir?*

Hope Bourne c 1920-

Self sufficient author / *Lives in Withypool*

A living legend on Exmoor, Hope Bourne has resided in several remote cottages and even a shepherd's caravan. She was once very self sufficient, kept chickens and had a

Winchester rifle for company, which she used to shoot rabbits. She contributed a weekly column to the *West Somerset Free Press* and articles to the *Exmoor Review*. She has also written several books: *Living on Exmoor, A little History of Exmoor, Wild Harvest, My Moorland Year*, often illustrating them herself.

Birdie Johnson 1944- *Lived near Winsford*

Birdie Johnson was brought up on a remote sheep farm on Exmoor and lived there for many years. Birdie specialises in oral history and on behalf of the Dulverton and District Civic Society, she travelled throughout Exmoor with her recorder, listening to people's life stories. This led to her remarkable book: *Reflections - life portraits of Exmoor* with photography by Mark Rattenbury. Birdie now lives in the High Weald of East Sussex.

20 BRIDGWATER: MERMEN, THE EUREKA MACHINE AND THE FIRING SQUAD

THREE VERY VARIED STORIES, including the only poet born in Somerset to be court-martialled and then shot by firing squad.

William Diaper 1685-1717

POET / Born in Bridgwater

The son of Joseph Diaper, William went to Balliol at the age of fourteen as a poor scholar. In 1709 he was ordained a deacon at Wells and became a curate in the parish of East Brent. He found this rather a trial and wrote a humorous but slightly disparaging poem about the area simply called *Brent* which describes the isolation

and inconvenience of the Somerset marshes in winter as well as the great flood of 1703. (It was only published in 1727 after Diaper's death.) He then took a curacy at Dean near Basingstoke and entered London literary society, albeit briefly. He became a friend and protégé of Jonathan Swift and is referred to several times in the Swift's *Journal to Stella*:

'Here is a young fellow has writ some Sea Eclogues, Poems of Mermen, resembling pastorals of Shepherds, and they are very

pretty, and the thought is new. Mermen are he-mermaids; Tritons, natives of the sea. Do you understand me? I think to recommend him to our Society to-morrow. His name is Diaper.'

Swift is referring to *Nereides*, published in 1712, where Diaper took pastoral poetry underwater populating the sea bed with sea gods, Tritons and nymphs. Mermaids replace shepherdesses and fishermen have become Mermen who cannot resist the call of the

sea. Diaper, who was thin, short and ill, was given the sum of £20 by Lord Bolingbroke for his efforts. Diaper also produced a translation of Horace and of a poem on sea fishing by Oppian. In 1713, he was living "in a nasty garret, very sick". He died four years later, aged 32. Diaper's reputation lay forgotten for over 200 years until the poet and critic Geoffrey Grigson wrote an essay on him in his book *The Harp of Aeolus* published in 1947.

113

lance-corporal under heavy fire. In April 1917 he was himself wounded. While recovering he wrote a damning attack on the way in which the war was being prolonged. This was read out in the House of Commons. Sassoon was then famously shunted off to Craiglockhart War Hospital, Edinburgh, suffering from shell-shock. It was here that he met Wilfred Owen and thus began a brief but intense poetic friendship, which led to the honing of many war poems which are still with us today. Sassoon was treated sympathetically by the psychologist W.H.R. Rivers who came to understand the underlying stresses and strains of shell shock. Both Sassoon and Owen returned to the Western Front. Sassoon was wounded again; Owen was killed. Sassoon's poems can be found in *The Old Huntsman* and *Counter Attack*.

After the war Sassoon became the first literary editor of the *Daily Herald* where he met Edmund Blunden. He wrote *Memoirs of a Fox-Hunting Man*, *Memoirs of an Infantry Officer* and *Sherston's Progress*. Other collections appeared: *Selected Poems*, *Satirical Poems* and *The Heart's Journey*.

In 1933 Sassoon married Hester Gatty and settled down at Heytesbury in Wiltshire where he lived for the rest of his life. Other books include *The Old Century* and *Seven More Years*, *The Weald of Youth* and *Siegfried's Journey*. He was appointed CBE in 1951, and was awarded the Queen's medal for poetry in 1957, the year that he became a Catholic. One of his delights was to take tea with Lord and Lady Oxford at Mells, driving over there in his 1933 Humber. When Sassoon died he was buried in Mells churchyard next to his good friend Ronald Knox.

To see: Sassoon's grave in Mells.

Monsignor Ronald Knox 1888–1957

PRIEST, CRIME WRITER AND BROADCASTER / Lived in Mells. Buried in Mells

Not a poet but a thriller writer. After Eton, Oxford and the First World War, Knox was destined not just for the Catholic Church but for a diverse career as a theologian and writer of crime novels. Maybe the two are not unconnected. His crime novels include *The Viaduct Murder, The Three Taps, The Footsteps at the Lock, The Body in the Silo, Still Dead* and *Double Cross Purposes*. His alter ego the detective was called Miles Bredon, employed by an insurance company.

Ronald Knox was one of the earliest BBC religious broadcasters. In 1926 he pulled off a great hoax. He pretended in a live report that a revolution was sweeping across London. This was entitled *Broadcasting from the Barricades* and by skilful mixing of sound, managed to convey over the radio that the Savoy hotel with its band music, was under attack from trench mortars and that its destruction was imminent. Many people were taken in for several days. Panic ensued. Recently it has been suggested that this gave Orson Welles the idea for his similar *War of the Worlds* broadcast.

Other works by Knox include *A Barchester Pilgrimage, The Scoop* and *Behind the Screen, Let Dons Delight* and *Enthusiasm*. He had a clear literary style and was even praised by the Pope.

Knox moved to Mells in 1947. He had been friends with Edward Horner who was killed in the First World War, and it was Edward's sister, Mrs Katharine Asquith, who invited Knox to live there. He stayed till he died in 1957. Interestingly one of Ronald Knox's brothers, Dilly Knox, worked in Room 40 in Naval Intelligence on decoding during the First World War and in 1937 Dilly broke the military codes used by Franco during the Spanish Civil War. During the Second World War he worked at Bletchley Park and successfully decoded the Italian naval code before Matapan. Another brother was a poet.

To see: His headstone and grave are in Mells.

Isaac Rosenberg 1890–1918

WAR POET AND ARTIST / Born in Bristol (see page 198)

John Jarmain 1911–1944

WAR POET / Lived at Pilton · Taught at Millfield

Of Huguenot descent, William John Fletcher Jarmain went to Cambridge and read mathematics. He then taught at Millfield School in Street and also gave lessons not just in maths, but in English, French and Italian. During the Second World War Jarmain joined up and served as an officer with the 51st Highland Division's anti-tank unit: 193 Bty, 61st Anti-Tank Regiment Royal Artillery. He served at Alamein and Tripoli in the Western Desert and in Sicily before returning to England. On D Day the 51st landed at Sword beach and then joined up with the 6th Airborne Division near Caen. Jarmain was killed by a German mortar–

bomb, before breakfast on 26 June 1944. He had gone forward on reconnaisance into Sainte Honorine la Chardonnerette, a rather fine village in the Calvados region east of the River Orne. His best known poems are *Embarkation*, *Prisoners of War* and *El Alamein*. In 1937 Jarmain wrote a novel about Mendip called *Priddy Barrows* which is about a year in the life of a school for disabled children on the Mendips, which was published in 1944. The editors of the wartime poetry collection *From Oasis into Italy* considered John Jarmain one of the truly great but neglected poets of the Second World War.

C.H. Sisson 1914-2003

POET, TRANSLATOR, NOVELIST AND CRITIC / Lived in Langport 1973-2003

Charles Sisson was born and brought up in Bristol where he gained a degree in English and philosophy. He entered the Civil Service in 1936 and during the Second World War, despite his fluency in French and German, he was sent to the North West Frontier, where in his spare time he translated and read Dante and Virgil. After the war he returned to the Civil Service, even writing a book on the subject *The Spirit of British Administration*. He also wrote a critical work called *The Case of Walter Bagehot*. Sisson was very fond of the classics; he produced many collections of essays and poems including *God Bless Karl Marx* and was an ardent critic. He moved to Langport in 1973 and lived there for 30 years Many of his poems describe the local area around Langport, notably: Aller Moor, Somerton Moor, Ham Hill, Muchelney Abbey and Athelney. He also wrote about Ellick Farm, near Burrington Combe where he spent time in his childhood. He was very good at translation and produced vigorous versions of Catullus, Lucretius, Dante's *Divine Comedy* , and Virgil's *Aeneid*. He had a long association with the Carcanet Press and Michael Schmidt. C.H. Sisson was made a Companion of Honour in 1993. His house Moorfield Cottage on The Hill, Langport, overlooked West Moor; in winter this often became a flooded landscape. He was a keen gardener and proud of his fruit trees. He is buried alongside his wife in Huish Episcopi graveyard.

John Mole 1941-

POET AND JAZZ CLARINETTIST / Born in Taunton. Lived in Kingston St Mary

John Mole grew up in Somerset and went to Bruton School and just by chance met John Steinbeck in the summer of 1959. As a school boy Mole, aged 17, wrote to the great author who was staying down the road at Discove and Steinbeck replied saying 'come along for a beer' which he did, with two of his friends. Bruton boys, beer and bicycles. John Mole has recorded this meeting eloquently in a poem called *The Other Day*. (Also, see Steinbeck page 128.)

John Mole is an accomplished poet and has produced more than fourteen volumes of poetry. He has also won several prizes: an Eric Gregory award, the Cholmondeley Award and the Signal Award. He has been Writer in Residence at Magdalene College, Cambridge and is currently the Poet in the City project's Poet in Residence to the City of London. His latest collection of poems is called appropriately enough *The Other Day*.

THE OTHER DAY — SUMMER 1959

Things like this happen, I suppose,
if you're young and lucky
and a reader. Also it helps perhaps
to be idolatrous. I was seventeen,

devouring all things USA in paperback
and dreaming of being Steinbeck
when the man himself arrived
at cycling distance from my school.
He and his wife had hired a cottage
for its local colour (this was the Vale
of Avalon) and he was here to work on
Malory's tales of Merlin and King Arthur.
Soon my own research came up
with an address. I wrote, and the reply
was friendliness, directions and a number.
Come over, he said, when I rang
from the dayroom payphone, telling him
how much I admired etc., breathless
at the drop of Button A, and mentioning
two fellow-fans. Why not bring them too
if your school will let you out. Say
Sunday afternoon if the weather holds
and we'll drink beer in the garden.

What do I remember? More than anything
that he wouldn't talk books. Through a cloud
of Capstan Navy Cut (I guess you boys
don't smoke and we pretended pusillanimously
to agree) he turned aside our tentative
interrogation, our admiring guff. Bob Hope
and Sergeant Bilko, how I love those guys.
I see they're on your network over here.
Who do you watch? And praise for Henry Fonda
was the nearest he came to mentioning
The Grapes of Wrath. His wife brought out
four bottles on a tray with secateurs
and gardening gloves, and everything
was all so obviously how they wanted it,
a rural idyll blessed by summertime
with old-world English schoolboys. Only, I recall,

one shadow when we touched on politics
and with a phrase which even now
brings back his living voice: John Foster Dulles
got your Suez business wrong, that man's
a mean hard-bitten Presbyterian.
I think I half-knew what he meant
and made a note of it to work in
somehow to a school debate, dropped casually,
As Steinbeck said to me the other day. . .

Why do I write this now? Because
(the other day) I was reading his biography*
and looked up Somerset for old time's sake.
So this had been a time when my hero's
work was going badly, and afterwards
it never picked up much, although announcement
of the Nobel had the happy couple
dancing round the room. But then
there was the story of his last hours
with his wife beside him. What would you say
was the best time we had in our
twenty years together? he asked. You first
she told him. No, I'm dying and you
would just agree with me. So what she did
was write down one word on a notepad,
tear the paper out and put it in his hand.
Now what was the best time we had?
and she didn't have to wait. Somerset, he said,
then opening up read SOMERSET in bold
and instant capitals, and so they lay together
reminiscing. . .

Sentimental? Yes. But allow me this,
the illusion of a possibility, that somewhere
in the images which returned for them
and now for me, three bicycles are leaning

by a cottage gate, the beer is carried out
across an English lawn, and an admiring
tongue-tied local schoolboy's politesse
turns down the offer of a cigarette.

*Jay Parini: John Steinbeck: a biography (Heinemann, 1994)

Lawrence Sail 1942-

Poet / *Lived in Roadwater*

Lawrence Sail was born in London and brought up in Exeter. His father was a well known painter, who came over from Germany in 1934. For many years he had a house in Roadwater. Lawrence went to Oxford and has had a career as teacher, poet and freelance writer. He has published nine collections of poems, including *Eye-Baby*, *The World Returning* and *Building into Air*. He has compiled and edited a number of anthologies, including *First and Always*: Poems for Great Ormond Street Children's Hospital and, with Kevin Crossley-Holland, *The New Exeter Book of Riddles* and *Light Unlocked*:

Christmas Card Poems. He has also had published *Cross-currents*, a book of his own essays. Over the years he has been chairman of the Arvon Foundation, programme director of the Cheltenham Festival of Literature and a judge for the Whitbread Book of the Year awards. In 1992 he was awarded a Hawthornden Fellowship, and in 2004 he received a Cholmondeley Award. He lives in Exeter.

Lawrence has three books awaiting publication in autumn 2010 - *Waking Dreams: New & Selected Poems*; *Songs of the Darkness: Poems for Christmas*; and *Running on Air*, a memoir of childhood.

ON PORLOCK BEACH

Do it once more. Lob the stone
you have just chosen - a layered chip
of Siena cathedral, green and whitish,
pummelled by pressures greater than Gothic -
and see it slither, mix to the mile-long
shelf of the foreshore.

Gone for ever - and no other stone
its exact equal. For sense you scan
the broader background, the curve of cliffs,
sea setting; eager to interpret
the laws of rhythm somewhere short
of never-never.

You harangue your heart, but cannot quench
a drowning desire to sense the single
in calm collectives; to let the beach
be each budding stone landing and lodging -
as judgements, whole with luck, but at least
tested by their parts.

22 THE NOVEL APPROACH – TWENTIETH CENTURY

MANY NOVELISTS have settled in Somerset at one time or another in the 20th century. They came from far and wide and each chose their own rural backwater to work in. Somerset would seem to be very conducive to writing. Some even came from as far afield as London and California.

Virginia Woolf 1882–1941

NOVELIST / Honeymoon in Wells · Lived in Holford

Virginia Woolf was born in London at Hyde Park Gate. Her father was Leslie Stephen and her mother Julia Duckworth. She had an unsettled upbringing and started to learn Greek, in between episodes of mental illness. Some academics think she was sexually abused by her half brothers. In 1908 she stayed in Wells at 9 Cathedral Green and 16 Vicar's Close and began writing her first novel, *The Voyage Out*, originally to be called *Melymbrosia*. She also left a description of Wells.

> *"I live in these lodgings about as near the sacred precincts as possible. Bells toll, & people shuffle down the Close to prayers. It is exactly the place in which some grey superstition should linger... The Cathedral of course dominates the whole place'*

(*A Passionate Apprentice*, 'Wells and Manorbier, August 1908')

Virginia Woolf once walked to Cheddar over Mendip and caught the train back. She did not like Cheddar Gorge and did not visit the caves. Of the gorge she said it would be 'alright for a switch-back ride'.

In 1911 she swam naked with Rupert Brooke at Grantchester and in August 1912 she married Leonard Woolf. They went first on their honeymoon to Holford in the Quantocks and stayed for three or four days at The Plough Inn. Virginia was not well and had psychological problems with eating. They then went to Europe for their main honeymoon. In the summer of 1913 Virginia had been working on many different drafts of *The Voyage Out* and had become very tired and agitated. They went away again to Holford in August for a rest, but it was not a success. The Woolfs then returned to London and a few days later Virginia attempted suicide. *The Voyage Out* was eventually published in 1915. Virginia then recovered and went on to write many other novels including *Mrs Dalloway, To the Lighthouse, Orlando, The Waves* and *The Years*. In 1917, the Woolfs also founded the Hogarth Press. In August 1940 their London house was bombed and they moved to Sussex where in March 1941 Virginia committed suicide by filling her overcoat pockets full of stones and so drowned herself in the river Ouse.

To visit: Wells and The Plough Inn, Holford.

John Steinbeck 1902–1968

AMERICAN NOVELIST / Lived near Bruton 1959

Steinbeck was born in California of joint German and Irish ancestry. He was one of America's most prolific writers in the twentieth century and is famous for his many novels, including *The Grapes of Wrath* for which Steinbeck won the Pulitzer Prize in 1939. During the Second World War he worked for the *New York Herald Tribune* as a war correspondent. In 1962 he won the Nobel Prize for Literature. His other works include *Of Mice and Men, East of Eden* and *Travels with Charley*.

What brought Steinbeck to Somerset was his fascination with the colourful character Thomas Malory (1415-1471) and his work *Le Morte d'Arthur* (see pages 14-16). These stories had captured Steinbeck's imagination since his ninth birthday, when his aunt gave him a book on the Arthur legends. Forty years later Steinbeck was determined to make a modern version of the Arthurian story based on the Winchester Manuscript which was re-discovered in 1934. He began work on his project in November 1956 and came to England in the summers of 1957 and 1958. In the winter of 1958/59, suffering from a bout of `writer's block', Steinbeck decided to return to England. In 1959 he came with his wife to Somerset and stayed nine months at Discove Cottage, Redlynch, just outside Bruton. The cottage had been found for him by Robert Bolt, a local teacher and playwright. As Steinbeck said himself 'It was a fortunate accident which drew me to this place. I am depending on Somerset to give me the something new which I need.'

"The countryside is turning lush as a plum. Everything is popping. The oaks are getting that red colour of swollen buds before they turn grey and then green. Apple blossoms are not out yet, but it won't be very long... Time loses all its meaning. The peace I have dreamed about is here, a real thing: thick as a stone and feelable and something for your hands."

Steinbeck obviously enjoyed his stays in Somerset and on his deathbed he then regarded it as some of the happiest times he had ever had. But sadly he had only completed seven chapters of his *magnum opus*. Also his literary agent and publishers didn't like it. It wasn't modern enough – so it was only published posthumously in 1976 as *The Acts and Deeds of King Arthur and his Noble Knights*.

To see: Steinbeck's writing desk is to be found in Bruton museum. See John Mole's Steinbeck poem: *The Other Day*.

Anthony Powell 1905-2000

NOVELIST / Lived at The Chantry, near Frome

The twelve novels published between 1951 and 1975 which make up the sequence *A Dance to the Music of Time*

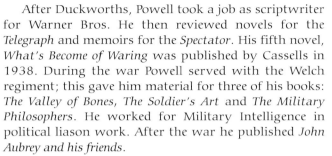

have been acclaimed as Powell's masterpiece and are regarded by some as the finest English fiction of the twentieth century. He is also seen by some as the English equivalent of Marcel Proust. The novels trace the fortunes of an eccentric group of English friends from 1914 to 1971, the most colourful being those set in the 1940s.

Powell went to Eton and Oxford where he met Evelyn Waugh and then worked for Duckworths the publishers. He was a frequent guest at Arthur Waugh's house on Sunday evenings in Hampstead. Evelyn also showed him the artistic, bohemian side of life at the Gargoyle Club in Soho. Powell's first novel, *Afternoon Men* was published in 1931. Within three years he had produced two more novels and got married to Lady Violet Packenham, (1912-2002), whose father was Thomas Packenham the Fifth Earl of Longford. She was herself a critic and writer. Her obituary in the *Telegraph* credits her as having 'rare intelligence, deftness, subtlety and oblique wit.' She is generally taken to be the model for the character of Isobel Tolland in *A Dance to the Music of Time*. She wrote three autobiographies as well as studies of Jane Austen, Somerville and Ross, Flora Annie Steel, Ivy Compton-Burnett, Margaret Kennedy and E.M. Delafield.

After Duckworths, Powell took a job as scriptwriter for Warner Bros. He then reviewed novels for the *Telegraph* and memoirs for the *Spectator*. His fifth novel, *What's Become of Waring* was published by Cassells in 1938. During the war Powell served with the Welch regiment; this gave him material for three of his books: *The Valley of Bones*, *The Soldier's Art* and *The Military Philosophers*. He worked for Military Intelligence in political liason work. After the war he published *John Aubrey and his friends*.

In 1950 he bought The Chantry, a Regency house near Frome, with its own grounds, a lake and two grottoes. Just the job for Somerset and round the corner from Mells. He then began writing his masterpiece. The title *A Dance to the Music of Time* was taken from Poussin's painting of the same name which he saw in the Wallace Collection in London. The novels in sequence are: *A Question of Upbringing*, *A Buyer's Market*, *The Acceptance World*, *At Lady Molly's*, *Casanova's Chinese Restaurant*, *The Kindly Ones*, *The Valley of Bones*, *The Soldier's Art*, *The Military Philosophers*, *Books Do Furnish a Room*, *Temporary Kings*, *Hearing Secret Harmonies*.

Powell also reviewed fiction for the *Times Literary Supplement*, the *Daily Telegraph* and the *Spectator*. In 1953 he became Literary Editor of *Punch*. When he died his ashes were scattered on the lake at The Chantry.

To see: memorial plaque in Chantry church, Whatley, west of Frome.

David Cornwell alias John le Carré 1931-

THRILLER WRITER / Lived at Coxley · Taught at Millfield

David John Moore Cornwell alias John le Carré was born in Poole, Dorset and was educated at Pangbourne and

Sherborne. He studied German at Berne and later worked in the British Army's Intelligence Corps in Austria. In 1952 he returned to England to study at Lincoln College, Oxford. When his father went bankrupt in 1954, le Carré had to leave Oxford to teach at Millfield. He later finished his degree and taught at Eton. He worked for MI5 and MI6 and started writing. In 1963 *The Spy Who Came in from the Cold* won him instant acclaim and the rest is history. George Smiley still rules a world littered with shadows and half shadows. Le Carré has written twenty one novels including *A Small Town in Germany*, *Tinker, Tailor, Soldier, Spy*, *The Honourable Schoolboy*, *Smiley's People*, *A Perfect Spy* and *The Constant Gardener*. Many of his books have been adapted for radio, film and television. He lived in Coxley for many years and then went to live in Cornwall.

Isabel Colegate 1931–

NOVELIST / Lived in Midford 1961-2007

Isabel Colegate was born in Lincolnshire. She moved to Midford with her husband Michael Briggs in 1961 and they then spent forty-five years restoring and living in Midford Castle, which was sold to Nicholas Cage in 2007. Isabel has written thirteen novels including *The Shooting Party* which won the 1981 WH Smith Literary Award. In 1985 it was made into a film which was directed by Alan Bridges and featured Sir John Gielgud, Edward Fox, James Mason and Dorothy Tutin. Isabel Colegate's other novels are: *The Blackmailer*, *A Man of Power*, *The Great Occasion*, *Orlando King*, *Orlando at the Brazen Threshold*, *Agatha*, *Deceits of Time*, and *Winter Journey*. She also wrote a book about hermits, solitaries and recluses, *A Pelican in the Wilderness*. She now lives in Mells.

Fay Weldon 1931–

NOVELIST / Lived in Pilton 1975-1990

The daughter of a doctor, Fay Weldon was born in Worcestershire but brought up in New Zealand. She returned to England on her fifteenth birthday. She comes from a writing family, her grandfather, mother and uncle all being novelists. Fay went to school in Hampstead and studied economics and psychology at St Andrews's University. She lived in Pilton for fifteen years. Fay has

Angela Coombes © Artists proof 1985 "Fay Weldon's Boys" Sam, Tom, Dan and Nick

written 32 novels to date including *Puffball* and *The Heart of the Country*, both set in Somerset. She started out as an advertising copy writer and famously, coined the phrase 'Go to work on an egg'. Perhaps not surprisingly this was to be the subject of one of her major novels – *The Cloning of Joanna May*. She tells me she also invented the pertinent slogan "Vodka makes you drunker quicker": alas, she wasn't allowed to use it.

Her first novel, *The Fat Woman's Joke*, was published in 1967. Other titles include *Down Among the Women*, *Female Friends*, *Praxis*, *The Life and Loves of a She-Devil*, *Wicked Women*, *Big Women*, *The President's Child*, *The Rules of Life*, *The Hearts and Lives of Men*, *The Shrapnel Academy*, *Rhode Island Blues*, *Mantrapped*, *She May Not Leave*, *What makes Women Happy*, *The Stepmother's Diary* and *Chalcot Crescent*. Nearly all have been translated abroad. She also writes for stage and screen, has many articles and short stories to her credit and an autobiography *Auto da Fay*. *Praxis* was short listed for the Booker Prize for Fiction. *Life and Loves of a She-Devil* was a major Hollywood production, *Puffball* was recently filmed by Nicolas Roeg. In 2001 she was awarded a CBE. In 2006 Fay Weldon was appointed Professor of Creative Writing at Brunel University, West London. She now lives in Dorset.

Penelope Lively 1933–

NOVELIST / Grandparents lived at Roadwater

Born in Cairo, Penelope Lively spent her childhood in Egypt and only came to England in 1945 after her parents' divorce. She was then aged twelve and one of her abiding memories is of Golsoncott, a large house near Roadwater in West Somerset, which belonged to her grandparents. Over the years she got to know the house very well and it must have been something of an anchor for her. *A House Unlocked* is set there; the story examines history room by room, object by object, the accumulation of memory. In the preface she sets out her aims: 'I thought that I would see if the private life of a house could be made to bear witness to the public traumas of a century'. *Going Back* is also about a country house in Somerset near Minehead. In this novel Golsoncott is called Medleycott. *Oleander, Jacaranda: A Childhood Perceived* is about her childhood in Egypt. She has written at least seventeen novels. *Moon Tiger* won the Booker Prize, *A Stitch in Time* won the Whitbread Award and *The Ghost of Thomas Kempe* won the Carnegie Medal. Penelope Lively has also written thirty children's books. Her latest novel *Consequences*, about three generations of women, is set in a small cottage in Somerset. West Somerset is often the backdrop for many of her stories, a rich tapestry that she uses adroitly. She was given a CBE in 2001.

Nell Dunn 1936–

NOVELIST AND PLAYRIGHT / Lived in Withiel Florey

Born in London, Nell Dunn went to a convent and later worked in a sweet factory. In the 1960s she wrote *Poor Cow* and *Up the Junction* which won the 1963 John Llewellyn Rhys Memorial Prize. *Poor Cow* was made into a film by Ken Loach starring Carol White and Terence Stamp. Then came *Grandmothers* and *My Silver Shoes* as well as a play called *Steaming*. In all she has written eight novels and seven plays, the latest of which is called *Cancer Tales*. In the 1970s Nell Dunn had a farm on Exmoor at Withiel Florey. It was through Nell that Margaret Drabble came to Exmoor. Both Nell and Margaret Drabble walked the Quantocks with Richard Holmes when he was researching his books on Coleridge. Nell Dunn was married to Jeremy Sandford.

Dame Margaret Drabble DBE 1939–

NOVELIST AND WRITER / Lives in Porlock

Margaret Drabble was born in Sheffield; her father was a barrister, judge and novelist. She went to a Quaker school in York, then Cambridge, where she gained a double First. Afterwards she joined the Royal Shakespeare Company. She has written seventeen novels including *The Witch of Exmoor*, a portrait of contemporary Britain set in London and Exmoor. Frieda Haxby Palmer is the eccentric present-day middle-class witch who can't abide 'things American.' The house, Exmoor and the coast along from Porlock Weir westward are symbols of escape for Frieda and some of her family.

Margaret Drabble's first novel, *A Summer Bird Cage*, was published in 1963. Her third novel, *The Millstone*, won her the John Llewellyn Rhys Memorial Prize and a year later she won the James Tait Black Memorial Prize with *Jerusalem the Golden*. Her other books include *The Waterfall*, *The Needle's Eye*, *The Realms of Gold*, *The Ice Age*, *The Middle Ground*, *Hassan's Tower*, *A Natural Curiosity*, *The Gates of Ivory*, *The Seven Sisters*, *The Red Queen* and *The Sea Lady*.

Margaret Drabble is patron and sponsor of the Porlock Arts festival which is held every year in September. She divides her time between London and Somerset. She is married to the biographer Sir Michael Holroyd. See page 154.

To visit: Porlock Arts Festival held every September.

Lindsay Clarke 1939–

NOVELIST / Lives in Frome

Lindsay Clarke's novel *The Chymical Wedding*, inspired by the life of Mary Anne Atwood, won the Whitbread Fiction Prize in 1989. John Fowles commented that it had 'excited him more than any other English fiction for some time.' Ted Hughes said that it was 'Full of wise things.' It has been translated into Swedish and Japanese.

Clarke's other novels are *Sunday Whiteman* and *Alice's Masque*. Lindsay was born in Halifax and educated at Heath Grammar School in Halifax and at King's College Cambridge. He worked in education for many years, in Africa, America and the UK, before becoming a full-time writer. He has also written *Essential Celtic Mythology*, *Parzival* and *The Stone from Heaven: A Grail Romance Retold for Our Time*, *The War at Troy* and *The Return from Troy*. He has also written four plays for BBC Radio Four. Lindsay Clarke lectures in creative writing at the University of Wales, Cardiff, and teaches writing workshops in London and Bath.

She has also written biographies of Arnold Bennett and Angus Wilson as well as critical studies of William Wordsworth and Thomas Hardy. She has also compiled *A Writer's Britain – Landscape and Literature* and has edited several editions of the *Oxford Companion to English Literature*. In 2008 *The Pattern in the Carpet: A Personal History with Jigsaws* was published.

PART FOUR

FROM WELLS TO MELLS

*Wells Cathedral
from a drawing by
John O'Connor,
engraved by
John Saddler*

27 BIOGRAPHERS AND DIARISTS

Delving into other people's lives is a fascinating occupation. Diaries and letters are incredibly useful to biographers because it is there that they often find the true thoughts and feelings of their subject. Biography often gives accurate insights into someone's state of mind at a particular time as well as the historical climate in which they lived.

Dr Claver Morris 1659-1727

DOCTOR, DIARIST AND MUSICIAN / Lived in Wells

Claver Morris came from Bishop's Caundle in Dorset and studied natural philosophy and medicine at Oxford. From the 1680s onwards he practised as a physician in Wells, sometimes travelling as much as 25 miles on horseback from Wells to see a patient. He lived in the Liberty, was a very keen amateur musician and married three times. The house that he built is now part of the Cathedral School. For many years Claver Morris was unknown outside Wells but in 1934 *The Diary of a West Country Physician, AD 1684-1726* was published. This gives a rare and early insight into a doctor's life in late Stuart and early Hanoverian England. Dr Claver Morris was buried in Wells Cathedral where, in the cloisters, there is now an elaborate memorial erected to his memory.

John Boyle 5th Earl of Cork and Orrery 1707-1762

BIOGRAPHER / Lived at Marston Bigot, near Frome

Born in London, Boyle went to Christ Church, Oxford, afterwards leading an unremarkable life in London as a politician in the House of Lords, dogged by his father's Irish debts. In 1745 he supported the Jacobite cause.

Much more important, however, was his friendship with Alexander Pope and Jonathan Swift, whom he first met in 1732. His best-known work is *Remarks on the Life and Writings of Dr Jonathan Swift* published in 1752. He also translated Horace's Odes and Pliny's letters and wrote *Letters from Italy* 1754-5.

Parson James Woodforde 1740-1803

DIARIST AND FOOD COMMENTATOR / Born Ansford, Castle Cary

James Woodforde was the son of the Rector of Ansford and Vicar of Castle Cary. He was educated at Winchester and New College. For ten years after graduation he worked as a curate for his father and at Thurloxton between Taunton and Bridgwater. His diary, which he kept for nearly 45 years, is peppered with down-to-earth observations about the Somerset people that he encountered every day, giving them nicknames such as Peter 'Cherry Ripe' Coles, 'Mumper' Clarke, 'Riddle' Tucker. The Ansford Inn and the George Inn in the

centre of Castle Cary is mentioned on many occasions as are the antics of his brothers who enjoyed cock-fighting. His entry for March 1st 1768 records the happenings at election time: *"Great dinners etc., given today at the George Inn. There were a great multitude of all sorts, gentle and simple. Bells ringing etc., and a great procession through Town with Musick playing and guns firing."* On July 2nd 1777 a crowd assembled at The George to see Robert Biggins lashed to a cart and whipped round the streets of the town for stealing potatoes. There was a collection of seventeen shillings and sixpence for the Hangman *"an old man and most villainous looking"* who did the whipping, but James Woodforde would have none of it.

In 1774 he was presented to the living of Weston Longville, Norfolk. Parson Woodforde never married but his niece Nancy Woodforde (1757-1830), born at Alhampton, Ditcheat, kept house for him in Norfolk. She also kept a diary and after her uncle's death came back to Castle Cary.

The Parson's diary was unknown until selections were published by Oxford University Press under the title *The Diary of a Country Parson* (Five vols: 1924-31). The MS Diary, consisting of 72 notebooks and 100 loose sheets, is deposited in the Bodleian Library, Oxford. A definitive edition has been published by the Parson Woodforde Society.

Parson William Holland 1746-1819

DIARIST / Lived in Over Stowey see page 69

Rev John Skinner 1772 - 1839

DIARIST AND ANTIQUARIAN / Born at Claverton, Lived at Camerton. See Eccentric Clergymen page 80

Robert Francis Kilvert 1840-79

DIARIST / Educated in Bath, visited Weston-super-Mare and Cheddar

Born near Chippenham in Wiltshire, Francis Kilvert was educated at Claverton Lodge School, run by his uncle Francis Kilvert. After Oxford, Kilvert became curate for his father at Langley Burrell; in 1865 he went to Clyro near Hay on Wye. In 1872 he returned to Langley Burrell; in 1877 he became vicar of St Harmon in Radnorshire and then finally vicar of Bredwardine in Herefordshire. He admired and visited the Dorset poet William Barnes, travelled on the Continent to France and Switzerland and was even offered the chaplaincy of Cannes. But in August 1879 he died of peritonitis, ten days after returning from his honeymoon in Scotland. His diaries recalling rural life in the Welsh Marches are now very well known, but were not published until 1938. He leaves accounts of bathing naked at Weston-super-Mare and visiting Gough's Cave at Cheddar. Sadly his family destroyed all but three volumes, his amorous and even erotic entries about some of his female pupils were considered too risqué for a wider audience.

John Bickersteth 1921–

DIARY EDITOR / Bishop of Bath and Wells

John Bickersteth edited the much acclaimed *Bickersteth Diaries 1914-18* which were published in 1996. These diaries were compiled initially by Ella Bickersteth, John's grandmother, from letters sent back to her from the Western Front by her six sons during the First World War as well as very frank letters exchanged between them. The original diaries run to eleven volumes of 3,000 pages. They give an extraordinarily honest appraisal of

29 SCIENCE FICTION, HUMOROUS PHANTASY AND HORROR

SOMERSET HAS BEEN HOME to many writers who wished to stretch the boundaries of our perception of both space and time. Some of them are now internationally known. Maybe it is the underlying history of non- conformity which stirs their imagination.

Arthur C. Clarke 1917-2008

SCIENCE FICTION WRITER AND FUTURIST / Born in Minehead

Arthur C. Clarke's mother, Nora Willis, was a butcher's daughter. Her grandfather was none other than Arthur Heal, a well-known huntsman for the Devon and Somerset Staghounds who was interviewed by Richard Jefferies in 1882 for his book on Exmoor and Red Deer. (see page 109.) Arthur C. Clarke's father came from Bishop's Lydeard where the family ran the Post Office for many years. Nora went to work there and married the son, Charles Clarke. Her son Arthur Charles Clarke was born in a guest house in Blenheim Road, Minehead, then run by her mother. After the war they farmed near Chard and then at Ballifants, near Bishop's Lydeard. Nora Clarke tells her own story about her family growing up in *My Four Feet on the Ground* published in 1978. Arthur went to school at Richard Huish in Taunton and built his first telescope when he was 13. He became fascinated by the Post Office and telecommunications. During the Second World War he worked in the RAF as a specialist in early warning radar defence. Later he obtained a First class degree in maths and physics at King's College, London.

Arthur C. Clarke contributed to many magazines including *Dan Dare*, stories for *Eagle*, and wrote a number of books about rocketry and space flight including *The Exploration of Space* and *The Promise of Space*. In 1945 he proposed a system of geo-stationary satellites upon which all modern communication systems are now designed. He was the chairman of the British Interplanetary Society from 1947-1950 and again in 1953.

His *2001: A Space Odyssey* was filmed by Stanley Kubrick, with whom he shared an Oscar nomination. Clarke's other novels include *Prelude to Space, Childhood's End, Rendezvous with Rama, A Meeting with Medusa, Songs of Distant Earth, The Fountains of Paradise, A Time Odyssey* with Stephen Baxter and *The Last Theorem* with Frederick Pohl. Clarke was also on good terms with CS Lewis.

Arthur C. Clarke moved to Sri Lanka in 1956 and ran a diving school. This was destroyed by the 2004 tsunami but has since been rebuilt. Arthur was always proud of his Somerset roots; he last visited Minehead in 1992 on his 75th birthday, when he was made the first Freeman of Minehead. He was given a knighthood by Prince Charles in 2000.

To see: Plaque at 13 Blenheim Road, Minehead.

John Brunner 1934–1995

SCIENCE FICTION WRITER / Lived in South Petherton

Born in Oxfordshire, John Brunner obtained a BA in modern languages at Oxford and was an officer in the RAF in the 1950s. He wrote more than 80 novels, often under pen names such as K. H. Brunner, Gill Hunt, John Loxmith, Trevor Staines and Keith Woodcott. His best known books are *Stand on Zanzibar, The Sheep Lock Up, The Jagged Orbit* and *The Shock Wave Rider*. Brunner is often credited with the invention of the term 'worm' or computer 'tape worm' in relation to a computer virus which reproduces itself, a term that is now in everyday use throughout the computer literate world. He lived in South Petherton for many years.

Terry Pratchett 1948–

FANTASY NOVELIST / Lived in Rowberrow

Terry Pratchett was born in Beaconsfield and lived briefly in Bridgwater in 1957. His earliest inspirations were *The Wind in the Willows* and the works of Isaac Asimov and Arthur C. Clarke. He was keen on astronomy and collected Brooke Bond tea cards on space. He started working as a reporter for the *Bucks Free Press* in High

Wycombe in 1965 and moved to Rowberrow near Shipham on Mendip in 1970 when he started work for the *Western Daily Press*. His first novel, *The Carpet People* was published a year later. This was followed by The *Dark Side of the Sun* (1976) and *Strata* (1981). In 1980 Pratchett became Press Officer for the Central Electricity Generating Board in an area covering three nuclear power stations, including Hinkley Point. No doubt he had to be skilful with his words. He is best known for his Discworld novels of which there are now thirty-seven . In 1993, the family moved to Wiltshire. His daughter Rhianna Pratchett is also a writer. In 2007 he was diagnosed with a rare variant of Alzheimer's disease, and has since then received wide support for his publicity and campaigning on behalf of those that suffer from Alzheimer's. Pratchett is one of the UK's best-selling authors: by the end of 2009 he had sold more than 65 million books worldwide, with translations in thirty-six languages. In 2009 he was knighted for his outstanding contribution to literature. His latest book, *Unseen Academicals*, was launched in autumn 2009 with a football tournament at Wincanton Sports Centre, hosted by Transworld Publishers. The Wincanton Urchins were jubilant winners of trophies presented by Sir Terry, celebrating with pies and cider all round.

To see: In 2002 Wincanton was officially twinned with the fictional city of Ankh-Morpork from the Discworld novels. Street names such as *Peach Pie Street* and *Treacle Mine Road* can be found at the Kingwell Rise development.

Kim Newman 1959–

JOURNALIST AND HORROR FICTION WRITER / Lived in Aller

Kim Newman was born in London and brought up in Aller. He was educated in Bridgwater. He wrote a semi-autobiographical account of this featuring a town called *Sedgewater*. He has written a series of *Warhammer* novels under the name of Jack Yeovil, as well as the *Anno Dracula* series. Kim has won the Bram Stoker Award, the International Horror Guild Award, the BSFA award, and has been nominated for the World Fantasy Award.

Tom Holt 1961–

NOVELIST / Lives in Chard

Tom Holt comes from 'genuine West Somerset stock; farm labourers in and around the Minehead area more or less since the Flood.' He works a smallholding and raises pigs and pedigree Dexter cattle. Also he is an Oxford graduate and has written a wide variety of satirical, humorous and historical books including *Who's Afraid of Beowulf, Open Sesame, Faust among Equals, Wish You Were Here, Snow White and the Seven Samurai, Nothing but Blue Skies* and *Barking*. He has also written *The Walled Orchard* and *Goatsong*, novels about ancient Athens, as well as *I, Margaret* a spoof autobiography, he co-wrote it with Steve Nallon of *Spitting Image* fame. His mother, Hazel Holt, is a novelist and still lives near Minehead. See page 222.

30 YEOVIL: HAND IN GLOVE

Today we think of Yeovil as being the home of helicopters and glove-making , but it also has many links to the world of books. Some regard Walter Raymond as Somerset's Thomas Hardy. The one unexpected find in Yeovil reference library was Harald Penrose who wrote about the magic of flight almost as eloquently as Antoine de Saint Exupery. John Cowper Powys set part of Wolf Solent in Yeovil and gave it the unenviable name of Blacksod. At least two of its MP's had Balkan connections: Aubrey Herbert who was offered the throne of Albania twice and Paddy Ashdown who is well known in Bosnia…

Walter Raymond 1852–1931

Novelist and historian / Born in Yeovil

Walter Raymond's father worked in the glove-making industry. When he was only two years old, Walter's mother and sister both died of typhoid and Walter, although very ill himself, was sent to live with his grandparents in Marston Magna. His father remarried; Walter continued to live in Yeovil but went to school in Sherborne. In 1878 Walter married Mary Johnston and continued his father's business, living in Vicarage Street, which has now been absorbed by the pedestrian precincts of the Quedam Centre.

In 1892 at the age of 40 Walter retired from the gloving business and began his literary career. He moved to Preston Plucknett, then to London but rented cottages first in Withypool and then in Nether Stowey. He finally ended up in Street and became good friends with the Clark family.

Walter Raymond's books often have specific Somerset locations in mind. They include *Misterton's Mistake*, *Under the Spreading Chestnut Tree*, about Marston Magna,

Taken at his Word, *Tryphena in Love*, *Gentleman Upcott's Daughter* set in Queen Camel, *Young Sam and Sabina*, set in Middleney. He also produced *The Book of Simple Delights* about Exmoor, and wrote *A Short History of Somerset*. His last novel, *Two Men of Mendip*, features the villages of Cheddar, Ubley, Shipham, Charterhouse and Winscombe

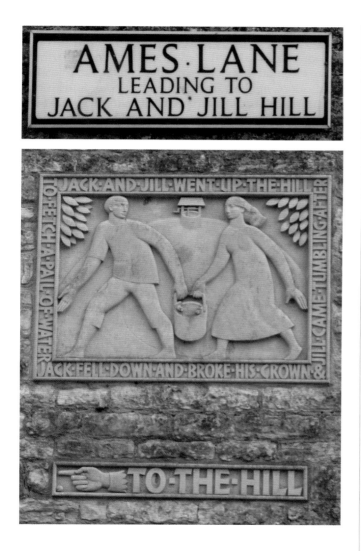

Jack and Jill Kilmersdon

The village of Kilmersdon has a long tradition of association with the nursery rhyme and the hill featured in the rhyme is said to be the very one in this village. Though what they were doing going up a hill to get a pail of water is slightly debatable.

To see: There are signs and murals, as well as a well, at the school which is, as you might expect, at the top of the hill.

Ring a Ring a Roses Holcombe

This is related to the plague when a posy of flowers was supposed to keep the evil smells of death away. The roses were the blotches on one's skin that marked the onset of the disease. 'At tishoo' ie sneezing was another symptom. Holcombe and many other villages claim to be the original village. Holcome is in fact a plague village, like Stoke Trister near Wincanton. The village moved a mile away, but the church stayed put. Melplash in Dorset also has a Posy Tree.

The Teddy Bear's Picnic Staplegrove

This children's song was written by James Jimmy Kennedy (1902-1984). He wrote many other popular songs, including *The Isle of Capri* and *Red Sails in the Sunset*. Kennedy is buried in Staplegrove churchyard and to raise money one year, the village arranged a 'death slide' for teddy bears, from the church tower to the graveyard below.

W.M.Thackeray, del.

PART FIVE

FROM CLEVEDON PIER TO CIDERLAND

From The Virginians
by William Makepeace
Thackeray

35 CLEVEDON — HONEYMOONS AND OTHER LIAISONS

C LEVEDON was one of the first seaside resorts in Somerset and drew many well-to-do people there on holiday or honeymoon. Writers particularly seemed to like its bracing Bristol Channel air. The attraction of staying at Clevedon Court was not to be underrated either, as Thackeray and Tennyson discovered.

Samuel Taylor Coleridge
1772-1834

POET / Honeymoon in Clevedon 1795

Coleridge rented a cottage at Clevedon overlooking the sea in August 1795. On October 4th the same year he married Sara Fricker at St Mary Redcliffe *'poor Chatterton's church.'* They had their honeymoon in Clevedon and stayed there for several months. Robert Southey married Sara's sister Edith Fricker soon afterwards, but they went to live in Portugal.

Coleridge wrote several poems here; *Effusion xxxv* a sonnet was composed on 20th August 1795 at Clevedon. *Eolian Harp* was probably written just before their marriage but it is very similar to *Effusion xxxv.*

COLERIDGE COTTAGE, CLEVEDON   57162

Coleridge also wrote another lesser known poem, *Lines Written at Shurton Bars*, in September 1795 to Sara, anticipating their imminent marriage and physical union. Shurton Bars is close to Hinkley Point nuclear power station, a local hot spot today. *Reflections On Having Left A Place Of Retirement* was written about Clevedon whilst in Bristol. *Silver Thimble* was written by Sara but with some help from Coleridge. Coleridge also edited a radical Christian journal, *The Watchman*, whilst he was in Clevedon. Their son Hartley Coleridge was born in 1796. Coleridge spent time in Bristol and then moved in 1797 to Nether Stowey. See page 58.

Arthur Hallam 1811–1833

Poet / Buried in Clevedon (see page 58)

Alfred Lord Tennyson 1809–1892

Poet / Visited Clevedon in 1850 (see page 119)

William Makepeace Thackeray 1811–1863

Novelist / Often stayed at Clevedon Court

Thackeray's father, Richmond Thackeray, was a writer with the East India Company – in other words a secretary, which was much more important than a mere clerk. In 1810 Richmond married Ann Becher, 'one of the reigning beauties of the day' in Calcutta. William was born there in 1811 and sent home to England at the tender age of five. He went to Cambridge and London and like many other potential writers studied law at the Middle Temple, but the strictures of the law were not for him. He went travelling on the Continent, gained his inheritance and squandered it on gambling and funding two unsuccessful newspapers. The rest of his fortune was lost in the collapse of two Indian banks.

He married and became a hack, writing for *Fraser's Magazine* and *Punch*. His early works include *Catherine*, *The Luck of Barry Lyndon* and *The Book of Snobs* as well as *The Paris Sketch Book* and *The Irish Sketchbook*. But the work which made his name was *Vanity Fair*, serialised in 1847. He wrote part of it at Clevedon Court as a guest of the Elton family. Sir Charles Abraham Elton, 6th Baronet, was himself a gifted writer who contributed to several periodicals including *The Gentleman's Magazine*. Thackeray was at Cambridge at the same time as Arthur Hallam, whose mother Julia Elton was Sir Charles's

sister. Thackeray had even poked fun at the Chancellor's Gold Medal whose subject in 1829 was *Timbuctoo*, a medal that was won that year by Tennyson.

The success of *Vanity Fair* was the character of Becky Sharp, a young woman who uses her wiles and manipulative feminine skills to climb the social ladder. A contrast to the usual 'virtuous angel', she scandalised and delighted Victorian readers.

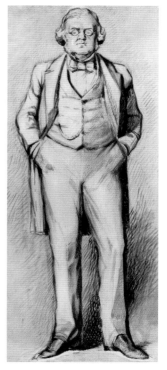

Sadly for Thackeray his wife suffered from terrible depression after the birth of their third child in 1840 and she never really recovered from it. She ended up being confined to a house outside Paris and outlived Thackeray by thirty years. Thackeray also wrote *Pendennis*, *The Newcomes*, and *The History of Henry Esmond* where Clevedon Court is portrayed as *Castlewood*. Thackeray, a big man in every sense, ate and drank to excess and had had a great liking for spicy peppers, a taste no doubt acquired in Calcutta.

To see: Portraits in the Thackeray Room at Clevedon Court and his quill writing pens.

THE GREEN BEACH.

[From a Photo. by Poulton & Son.

George Gissing 1857-1903

NOVELIST / Visited Clevedon 1888, 1891 and 1894

Gissing used Clevedon as the setting for *The Odd Women*, and it is mentioned in *The Private Papers of Henry Ryecroft*. Gissing returned here in 1894 with his family and worked on *Eve's Ransom*. He visited Weston-super-Mare and went by train to Minehead, which he described as 'a terrific experience'. He also visited Watchet as well as taking a steamer trip round the lightships.

George Gissing was born in Wakefield and won a scholarship to Owen's College in Manchester. Here he was caught stealing from his fellow students. The reason was that he had fallen in love with a prostitute called Marianne and wanted to support her by any means. Convicted of theft he was sentenced to one month's hard labour in prison. He then went to America and started writing short stories for the *Chicago Tribune*. He returned in 1877 and went to live in London. He married Marianne and started his writing career in earnest. Sadly she became an alcoholic and died in 1888. His first book was called *Workers in the Dawn*. He also wrote *The Nether World*, *New Grub Street* and *Born in Exile*. In 1893 *The Odd Women* was published. This was followed by *Eve's Ransom*. His other books include *In the Year of Jubilee*, *The Whirlpool* and a largely autobiographical work called *The Private Papers of Henry Ryecroft*, from which the following extract is taken:

"I have been spending a week in Somerset. The right June weather put me in mind for rambling, and my thoughts turned to the Severn Sea. I went to Glastonbury and Wells and on to Cheddar, and so to the shore of the Channel at Clevedon, remembering my holiday of fifteen years ago, and too often losing myself in a contrast of the man I was then and what I am now. Beautiful beyond all words of description that nook of oldest England; but that I feared the moist and misty winter climate, I should have chosen some spot below the Mendips for my home and resting place. Unspeakable the charm to my ear of those old names; exquisite the quiet of those little towns, lost amid tilth and pasture, untouched as yet by the fury of modern life, the ancient sanctuaries guarded, as it were, by noble trees and hedges overrun with flowers. In all England there is no sweeter and more varied prospect than that from the hill of the Holy Thorn at Glastonbury; in all England there is no lovelier musing place than the leafy walk beside the Moat at Wells. As I think of golden hours I spent there, a passion to which I can give no name takes hold of me; my heart trembles with an infinite ecstasy."

George Gissing died in December 1903 aged 46 from the effects of emphysema. He had two sons, Walter Gissing and Alfred Gissing. Walter trained as an architect but was killed at the Battle of the Somme in 1916. Alfred survived the war and became a writer and headmaster of a school in Switzerland. The novelist and writer Algernon Gissing (1860-1937) was George Gissing's elder half-brother.

Rupert Brooke 1887-1915

POET / Spent a summer holiday in Clevedon 1909

Rupert Brooke was born at Rugby where his father taught. Brooke was very much an all rounder, played cricket and rugby as well as writing poems. Thence to King's College, Cambridge, where he read Classics. Brooke moved in interesting circles where one's sexuality was always open to interpretation. First he was attracted to boys, which was quite the norm at public school, but then in 1908 he fell in love with a fifteen-year-old schoolgirl called Noel Olivier who had just started at Bedales. This was the era of so called neo-pagan long

36 BRISTOL ROVERS

ALTHOUGH BRISTOL is not strictly Somerset it is included for several reasons. For a thousand years or more all the land south of the river Avon was in Somerset, so most of South Bristol today was historically part of Somerset. Secondly, many of the Somerset writers spent time in Bristol or like Robert Southey, were born there. Like Bath, Bristol was a centre for culture and had its own theatre, The Theatre Royal, which opened in 1766. More importantly Bristol was a large port and a melting pot of travels, trade and daring adventures. Many writers made significant friendships there, Wordsworth first met Coleridge in 7 Great George St Bristol. Many stories were exchanged on the quayside pubs. Defoe apparently heard first hand Alexander Selkirk's story in the Llandoger Trow. It was also the home base of Woodes Rogers and Shelvocke whose stories inspired Coleridge. Also, on a personal note, I lived in Bristol 1972-80, studied civil engineering and then worked in the docks for two summers as a ferryman and a narrow boatman on the Bristol Packet. On a purely technical note, most of the cider consumed in Bristol, which no doubt fuelled many of the more imaginative and vivid stories, would have been made in Somerset and sold in the numerous cider houses. Until 2003, at Long Ashton, Bristol had its very own Cider Research Station known as LARS. Their 'testing' days were famous.

Richard Hakluyt 1553-1616

GEOGRAPHER AND TRANSLATOR / Prebend of Bristol Cathedral 1586-1616

Richard Hakluyt came from a Herefordshire family and his father was a member of the Worshipful Company of Skinners which dealt with furs as well as skins. Hakluyt was born in London and educated at Christ Church Oxford. His important works of discovery and travel are well known. His first known work was published in 1582: *Divers Voyages Touching the Discoverie of America and the Ilands Adjacent unto the Same, Made First of All by Our Englishmen and Afterwards by the Frenchmen and Britons: With Two Mappes Annexed Hereunto.*

In 1584 another work was commissioned by Sir Walter Raleigh: *A Particuler Discourse Concerning the Greate Necessitie and Manifolde Commodyties That Are Like to Growe to This Realme of Englande by the Westerne Discoueries Lately Attempted.* He then spent five years in France and in 1589 published his major work: *The Principall Navigations, Voiages, and Discoveries of the English Nation: Made by Sea or Over Land to the Most*

CLIFTON AND ST VINCENT'S ROCKS WITH LEIGH WOODS.

apprenticeship before the mast in 1704 and must have seen action against the French and Spanish. In 1705 he married Sarah Whetstone daughter of Admiral Sir William Whetstone of Bristol, commander-in-chief in the West Indies. Woodes Rogers must have been very well respected for he was asked by William Dampier to command two vessels for another voyage round the world with Dampier as sailing master. The vessels were called *Duke* and *Duchess*. Many problems arose, including the desertion of 40 members of the crew from Bristol.

They had an uneasy voyage and were driven to 62 degrees latitude. In January 1709, as they neared Juan Fernandez island, they spotted smoke rising from a fire. Upon sending a party ashore they discovered Alexander Selkirk, a wild-looking man wearing goatskins, who had been marooned there at his own request by Dampier four years previously. This incident became the main inspiration for *Robinson Crusoe* written by Rogers's friend, Daniel Defoe. They then carried on their trade of piracy against the Spanish. One of the men who commanded a captured vessel was Simon Hatley, who later went around the world with Captain Shelvocke and shot the albatross whilst marooned in bad weather, (see below.)

Upon his return Woodes Rogers went back to Bristol and wrote his famous book *A Cruising Voyage Round the World* in 1712. Rogers led another expedition financed by the East India Company in 1713 to Madagascar to investigate the piracy there and to persuade them to renounce their unhealthy trade. In 1718 he was back in the West Indies as Captain General and Governor in Chief of the Bahamas, his task to reclaim the islands which had become 'infested' with pirates. He was up against Charles Vane and Edmund Teach alias Blackbeard, another Bristol sea captain who had gone native. Some pirates were pardoned, others were executed or flogged if they changed sides too often. Woodes Rogers slowly brought the Bahamas under the King's rule and restored order.

In 1723, Rogers was approached by a man interested in writing about the history of piracy. Woodes Rogers obliged and gave him much information. The resulting work, *A General History of the Robberies and Murders of the Most Notorious Pyrates* was published in 1723. It had been written under the pseudonym of Captain Charles Johnson. Many have supposed that he was none other than Daniel Defoe. Charles Johnson was a playwright who had written a rather lightweight play which had flopped in 1712 called *The Successful Pyrate* about the life of Plymouth-born pirate Henry Avery. Avery also went under the names of Long Ben and Benjamin Bridgeman. Reputedly he was the first pirate to fly the Jolly Roger. In 1728 Woodes Rogers was appointed Governor of the Bahamas for a second term and he died there in 1732.

In January 2009 an original 1712 copy of *A Cruising Voyage Round the World* was discovered in a Bristol loft and auctioned for £6,000.

To see: There is a blue plaque where his house stood in Queen Square Bristol. Woodes Rogers gave a pair of silver candlesticks to Bristol Cathedral as part of the treasure trove that he brought back.

Captain George Shelvocke 1675-1742

PRIVATEER AND AUTHOR CAPTAIN OF THE SPEEDWELL / Based in Bristol

Born in Shropshire, George Shelvocke joined the navy in 1690 when he was 15. He served in the French and Spanish wars and rose to be a second lieutenant under Admiral Benbow in the West Indies. After hostilities finished in 1713 he was put ashore on less than half pay. In 1719 Shelvocke was employed again as the captain of the Bristol-based *Speedwell* to accompany another vessel, the *Success*, commanded by John Clipperton. They were financed by Bristol merchants and their brief was to circumnavigate the globe. They were given leave to become privateers with the standard issue of letters of marque. Shelvocke was very much the pirate and went his own way. In May 1720 the *Speedwell* was wrecked on Selkirk Island. They built a boat from rescued timber and continued their piracy up the Chilean and Californian coasts before crossing to Macao and eventually reaching England. Upon his return Shelvocke was tried for piracy but was acquitted. He then wrote *A Voyage Round the World By Way of The Great South Sea* 1719-21. The book, written in 1723 was read by Coleridge seventy five years later. In it there is an account of Simon Hatley shooting down a black albatross that had dogged the ship when it was becalmed: a key feature of the *Ancient Mariner*. See also Coleridge page 58.

Edmund Burke 1729-1797

AUTHOR, ORATOR AND PHILOSOPHER / MP for Bristol 1774 -1780

He lived at 19 Queen Square. There is a bronze statue of Edmund Burke in Colston Avenue. In 2008 someone took a few pot-shots at the statue. See page 42.

William Combe 1741-1823

POET AND AUTHOR / Born in Bristol

William Combe was adept as a poet but also adept at getting into debt. He went to Eton and was on good terms with Charles James Fox, Baron Lyttelton and William Beckford. He was also influenced by the work of Lawrence Sterne. Count Combe, as he was known, lived life to the full. In 1775 he wrote *The Philosopher* in Bristol. A year later he made his first success in London with *The Diaboliad*. He also wrote *A Devil on Two Sticks in England*, and the very popular *Three Tours of Dr. Syntax* which included Dr Syntax in search of the Picturesque, followed by *The English Dance of Death*, *The Dance of Life*, *Picturesque Tours along the Rhine and other rivers*, *Historys of Madeira* and *Antiquities of York*.

Hannah More 1745- 1833

WRITER, POET, SOCIAL IMPROVER, MORALIST, EDUCATOR AND BLUE-STOCKING / Born in Bristol · Lived in Wrington · Died in Clifton

Hannah More was born at Fishponds on the outskirts of Bristol; her father was a schoolmaster at Stapleton. As a teenager she helped her sisters in a small boarding school run by the eldest: first in Trinity St and then at 43 Park Street. She started writing plays. The first, called *The Search for Happiness*, was first performed in 1762. In 1767 she was engaged to be married to Mr Turner of Wraxall, (next door to Tyntesfield) but it never came to fruition though Hannah did receive an annuity from him of £200 a year, a very useful sum which enabled her to continue writing. She went to London where she became a star of the literary world, admired by David Garrick, Samuel Johnson, Horace Walpole and Edmund Burke. She wrote several dramas and poems. The prologue and epilogue to her tragedy *Percy* was written by Garrick himself.

In Bristol she discovered the milkmaid poet Ann Yearsley and helped publish her work. Then in 1782 Hannah published *Sacred Dramas* which went into nineteen editions.

In 1785 she bought a house at Wrington, first at Cowslip Green and then at Barley Wood. She lived in the village for 42 years. See page 83. In the last five years of her life Hannah moved to Clifton and lived at 4 Windsor Terrace, but when she died she was buried at All Saints' Church, Wrington.

To see: Statue in porch of Wrington church and her grave in graveyard. There is a portrait of her in the Georgian House in Great George Street.

Thomas Chatterton 1752–1770

POET / Born in Bristol · Committed suicide with arsenic

The short life of Thomas Chatterton has intrigued poets and biographers alike. Born at the schoolhouse in Pile Street, he grew up in the shadow of St Mary Redcliffe which according to Elizabeth I, was 'the finest parish church in all of England'. Thomas Chatterton's father, who was a schoolmaster and sub-chanter at the church died shortly before Thomas's birth. His uncle was the sexton and it was here over the north porch, as Thomas read old manuscripts in the muniment room, that he gained his fascination for old lettering and language, ideas that later formed not just into poetry but into forgery as well. When he was about ten he started writing poetry; when he was nearly twelve he presented his friend Thomas Phillips with his first forged poem. At fifteen Chatterton left Colston's School to be apprenticed to an attorney called John Lambert. By 1768 a local magazine was accepting his 'medieval' poems as genuine: poems that he claimed he had found in St Mary Redcliffe. He even managed to fool a local historian called William Barrett. By then Chatterton was in touch with Horace Walpole whose Gothic novel *The Castle of Otranto* had come out in 1764. Chatterton by this time had taken on the persona of Sir Thomas Rowley a priest living around 1464 and wrote many poems as if he was Rowley himself, notably *Aella* and *An Excelente Balade of Charitie*. Walpole was suspicious but only suspected that Chatterton was after money. He returned the manuscripts. Chatterton wriggled out of his apprenticeship and went to London to seek his fortune. He stayed with relatives, then found a garret for himself in Holborn and worked as a

REDCLIFF CHURCH,
Briſtol.

London Published by Vernor & Hood Poultry May 1.1802.

jobbing hack. He pretended that he was successful but in reality he was starving. In August 1770 he took a mixture of arsenic and water. There is even a suspicion that he had a touch of gonorrhoea, in which case arsenic was a recognised cure, so he had access to the poison. He was a fine poet and his poems and desperate story fired the imagination of the Romantics.

To see: St Mary Redcliffe church.

Ann Yearsley c1753–1806

LACTILLA – THE MILKMAID POET / *Lived in Bristol*

Anne's mother was a milkwoman; she herself married a yeoman called John Yearsley in 1774. Years later the family hit hard times and Ann's poetry was noticed by Hannah More who helped her to publish them. With the timely proceeds Ann ran a circulating library in Hotwells, but she fell out with Hannah More, who insisted on paying her an annuity rather than letting her have the money all at once. One account says that the library folded and Ann Yearsley became increasingly unstable. She did, however, keep writing poetry this time supported by the Fourth Earl of Bristol. In 1778 she wrote a poem against *The Inhumanity of the Slave Trade*, and then turned to drama and even novel writing. Her last collection of poems, *The Rural Lyre* appeared in 1796. She died in Melksham.

Mary Robinson 1757–1800

POET, NOVELIST AND ROYAL MISTRESS / *Born in Bristol*

Mary's father was a sea captain called John Darby who deserted her mother, Hester, when the children were but young. To survive they started a family school. Mary was noticed by Hannah More, who introduced her to the actor David Garrick. She married an articled clerk called Thomas Robinson who claimed he was owed an inheritance. The couple fled to Wales, where he was imprisoned for debt and then eventually Mary came to the attention of Georgiana, Duchess of Devonshire, who funded the publication of her first volume of poetry called, aptly enough, *Captivity*. Returning to London, Mary played at Drury Lane. Her moment came in 1779 when as Perdita in *The Winter's Tale* she came to the attention of the Prince of Wales, the future George IV, who offered her £20,000 to become his mistress. An offer she couldn't exactly refuse. Sadly he took advantage of her but did not hand over the money. She was 'ruined' as they say, but in return for the Prince's love letters she was given £5,000. Not a bad deal in the circumstances. After several other affairs Mary Robinson became ill and in 1783 was partially paralysed. She continued to earn her living by writing poetry, plays and novels. She deserves to be better known.

Dr Thomas Beddoes 1760–1808

PHYSICIAN AND SCIENTIFIC WRITER / *Lived in Bristol, died in Bristol*

Born in Shropshire, Thomas Beddoes went to Oxford and then Edinburgh Universities. In 1784 he translated the work of the Italian naturalist and physiologist Lazzaro Spallanzani. Beddoes was interested in both medicine and chemistry and he met Lavoisier when he visited Paris. In 1793 he came to Bristol and published *The History of Isaac Jenkins*, a story which deplores the evils of drink, cider no doubt included. It sold over 40,000 copies. He conceived an Enlightenment idea of social medicine. He was also a friend of James Watt; together they saw science as the saviour of the poor and a weapon against the corrupt social order of the times. A year later he married Anna Edgeworth, sister of the novelist Maria Edgeworth. Dr Beddoes, with his republican views, soon became acquainted with the coterie of Romantic poets and their scientific adventures. He lived at 11 Dowry Square and in 1799 moved to 6 Dowry Square to join Humphry Davy, the Cornish engineer and pioneer of the Davy Lamp. They worked at the Pneumatic Institute where they used gases to cure diseases. Their assistant was none other than Peter Mark Roget 1779- 1869, the lexicographer who wrote *Roget's Thesaurus*. They also experimented not just with words but with nitrous oxide, otherwise known as Laughing Gas. Wordsworth and Coleridge famously experimented with laughing gas. By 1802 the Pneumatic Institute became the Preventive Medical Institution for the Sick and Drooping Poor. Beddoes wrote several books on the social aspects of medicine, namely *Hygeia and The Manual of Health* as well as *Observations on the Nature and Cure of Calculus*, *Sea Scurvy*, *Consumption*, *Catarrh, and Fever*. His son Thomas Lovell Beddoes was a 'Gothick' poet and dramatist.

Maria Edgeworth 1768-1849

NOVELIST / Lived in Clifton 1791-1799

Maria Edgeworth was born in Oxfordshire but grew up in England and Ireland where her family had estates. At one time she managed these for her father, gaining insights into a man's world. She also spent much time in Bristol at 3 Rodney Place in Clifton as her sister had married Dr.Thomas Beddoes. Two of her children's stories are set in Bristol: *The Parent's Assistant* and *Moral Tales*. Her other works include *Practical Education*, *Letters for Literary Ladies*, *Castle Rackrent*, her first novel, which was

Maria Edgeworth

From the original painting by Chappel in the possession of the publishers

followed by *Belinda*, *The Absentees*, *Patronage*, *Harrington*, *Ormond and Helen*, as well as various memoirs and comic dramas. An immensely popular writer in the nineteenth century. She died in County Longford, Ireland.

37 EGYPT AND ASSYRIA

Unlikely subjects for Somerset, but here are three very distinguished writers who made Egypt and ancient languages their speciality.

Thomas Young 1773-1829

Scientist, linguist and Egyptologist / Born in Milverton

Thomas Young was a bright lad. His father was a cloth merchant and banker and his mother came from Minehead. He went to a small Quaker school in Compton Abbas in Dorset and by the time he was fourteen he had learnt Greek and Latin as well as having a working knowledge of twelve other languages including Hebrew, Arabic, Persian, Turkish and Chaldean. He studied in London, Edinburgh, Gottingen and Cambridge. He set up as a doctor in London and in 1801 was appointed professor of Natural Philosophy at the Royal Institution. His lectures were published in 1807. In 1811 he was physician at St George's Hospital. His scientific experiments were important particularly with the wave theory of light and colour perception as well as the first description of astigmatism. He even invented Young's modulus in relation to elasticity which is applicable to all springs. His medical writings include *An Introduction to Medical Literature* and *A Practical and Historical Treatise on Consumptive Diseases*. He also devised a formula for determining the doses of certain drugs for children, which was the adult dosage multiplied by the child's age and then divided by twelve. He also devised various formulas to do with capillary action, surface tension and surface energy. In 1818 Young was appointed superintendent of the Nautical Almanac and secretary of the Board of Longitude.

His interest in languages however remained undiminished and his article in the *Encyclopaedia Britannica* compared over 400 languages. He coined the term 'Indo-European' languages. His main challenge,

CLEANING THE COLOSSUS.

however, was Egyptian hieroglyphics and the Rosetta Stone which had been found by the French in 1799. With the French scholar Jean-François Champollion he deciphered the stone. It turned out to be a decree from Ptolemy V describing the repealing of various taxes and instructions to erect statues in temples, with the same text written in Greek and hieroglyphics. This provided the key which enabled him to unlock the linguistic code. Young published several papers on the subject. At the time of his death he was working on an Egyptian dictionary. The Rosetta Stone has been in British Museum since 1802.

Edwin Norris 1795-1872

LINGUIST AND ASSYRIOLOGIST / Born in Taunton

The son of a Taunton printer, Edwin Norris attended the local school in Taunton where the headmaster was his uncle, a noted linguist who could speak 24 languages. Norris went to the Continent as a tutor and learnt Italian, Greek, Hebrew and Armenian. He returned to Taunton in 1821 and taught languages until 1826 when he went to London and was employed as a junior clerk in the East India Company. Here he learnt South Asian languages and Sanskrit. In 1836 he became secretary of the Royal Asiatic Society and learnt to decipher Old Persian and Babylonian cuneiform texts, as well as proclamations in Bactrian script from the time of Ashoka. For nearly ten years he assisted Henry Rawlinson in his publication *Cuneiform Inscriptions of Western Asia* and compiled his own Assyrian Dictionary, which was never finished due to his poor health and deteriorating eyesight. Norris wrote many other linguistic papers and books on African languages. He also undertook translation work for the Foreign Office and spoke Berber and Arabic as well as

Maori. Some regard his most important work, however, to do with Cornwall. In 1859 Norris published the *Ancient Cornish Drama* a trilogy of plays called the *Ordinalia*, which he translated from the fifteenth-century Oxford manuscript. The three mystery plays are *Origo Mundi- the Origin of the World, Passio Christi - the Passion of Christ* and *Resurrexio Domini - the Resurrection of Our Lord*.

Amelia Edwards 1831-1892

NOVELIST, JOURNALIST AND EGYPTOLOGIST / Died in Weston-super-Mare

Amelia was born in Islington. Her father was an army officer on half pay and her mother Alicia was connected to the Walpole family. Amelia, an only-child, was tutored at home. She read widely and started writing, early: her first poem was published when she was only seven and her first story when she was twelve. By the age of fourteen her work was being published in periodicals such as *Chamber's Journal, Household Words* and *All the Year Round*. Later she wrote for the *Saturday Review* and the *Morning Post*.

Between 1855 and 1880 she published eight novels. These included *My Brother's Wife*, *In the Days of my Youth* and *Barbara's History*, a novel of bigamy, that solidly established her reputation as a novelist. Her last novel in 1880, *Lord Brackenbury* went into 15 editions. She also published *Monsieur Maurice*, a collection of stories, and translated *A Lady's Captivity among Chinese Pirates* from the French as well as writing an English and French history. In 1864 she moved to Westbury-on-Trym, near Bristol. She travelled to Italy with a friend called Lucy Renshawe and together they explored the Dolomites. Amelia wrote this up in *Untrodden Peaks and Unfrequented Valleys*.

In 1873 they decided to go to Egypt together and made a tour with some friends. Amelia visited Abu Simnel and even helped to discover an unknown sanctuary. She was by then hooked. In 1876 she published *A Thousand Miles up the Nile* with her own hand-drawn illustrations. It became a best seller. By 1882 Amelia became aware of the need to protect monuments from excess tourism and vandalism, so she co-founded the Egypt Exploration Fund and worked with the British Museum. In 1889 she went on a lecture tour of the United States, in five months addressing some 100,000 people at about 110 meetings. These talks were published in a book called *Pharaohs, Fellahs, and Explorers*. She contributed and an article on Egypt to the ninth edition of the *Encyclopaedia Britannica* supervised by Thomas Baynes (see page 146).

In October 1891 she contracted a lung infection whilst supervising Egyptian antiquities arriving at London docks. She became increasingly ill and eventually died at 31 Royal Terrace, Weston-super-Mare. She is buried in the churchyard of St Mary, Henbury, near Bristol; her grave is marked by an obelisk.

38 DIGGING DEEP – ENTRENCHED ARCHAEOLOGISTS

I T IS OFTEN THE TASK of archaeologists and historians to piece together the past and it is their findings that often give writers the accuracy and information that they so desperately need. The painstaking work of interpreting the results from an archaeological dig is akin to doing a jigsaw with three-quarters of the pieces missing. Like novelists, archaeologists and historians have to reconstruct believable scenes and characters, as well as being able to project themselves into another time scale and geographical dimension. Reality in Somerset is often stranger than fiction.

Arthur Bulleid
and Harold St George Gray

ARCHAEOLOGISTS / Excavated at Glastonbury and Meare

Bulleid and Gray became famous for their excavations of the Glastonbury Lake Village which they undertook between 1892 and 1907. The village was close to Godney. The remains of the Iron Age village were found to be on top of a man-made island. Arthur Bulleid was the son of a local mayor and founder of the Glastonbury Antiquarian Society. He was a medical student and an amateur archaeologist. Harold St G Gray had been assistant and secretary to the well known Dorset archaeologist General Pitt-Rivers as well as curator of the Taunton Museum. Their reports were published by the Glastonbury Antiquarian Society in 1911 and 1917. They had uncovered a very sophisticated Iron Age culture which had links to the La Tene culture in Switzerland. From 1910 onwards they also excavated a similar lake village site at Meare. Their book describing the excavations and the relics from the eastern half of the west village, called *The Meare Lake Village* 1910-1933,

was privately printed at Taunton Castle in three volumes. Some of these reports can now be read online.

To see: Exhibition in The Tribunal in Glastonbury. Sadly the Peat Moors Visitor Centre at Westhay has now closed.

Ralegh Radford 1900-1999

ARCHAEOLOGIST AND HISTORIAN / Excavated in Glastonbury

Ralegh Radford went to Oxford and later pioneered the exploration of the Dark Ages of Britain. He made much of his work accessible through very well written and researched official guides. His excavations at Glastonbury were undertaken in the 1960s. The relevant books are: *Glastonbury Abbey - the Isle of Avalon*, *The Pictorial History of Glastonbury Abbey*, *The Quest for Arthur's Britain* and *Arthurian Sites in the West* which was a joint production. He also excavated at Tintagel. For his ninetieth birthday a volume of essays was produced in his honour: *The Archaeology and History of Glastonbury Abbey*. He retired to Uffculme.

Leslie Alcock 1925-2006

ARCHAEOLOGIST / Excavated at South Cadbury

Leslie Alcock was a well respected archaeologist who excavated South Cadbury hill fort in the 1960s. He went to Manchester Grammar School and served as captain in the Gurkhas in the Second World War. He read Modern History at Oxford, then worked under Sir Mortimer Wheeler at Mohenjodaro and went back to Pakistan as head of Archaeology. He also worked for 20 years as lecturer and Reader at Cardiff University. It was at this time that he excavated at South Cadbury. His dig became very well known and attracted many visitors. His summary report was published in 1967. Alcock also wrote *Was This Camelot? Excavations at Cadbury* and *Arthur's Britain*. Later Leslie Alcock became Professor of Archaeology at Glasgow University.

Mick Aston 1946-

FIELD AND LANDSCAPE ARCHAEOLOGIST / Lives in Winscombe

Mick Aston is well known from the Channel 4 *Time Team* programmes. shown on television. Before that he was attached to Birmingham University and also taught extra-mural courses at Oxford. He became Somerset's first County archaeologist and was based in Taunton. He also taught at Bristol University. The first *Time Team* programe went out in 1994 and since then they have gone from strength to strength. Mick Aston ran the Shapwick project with Professor Chris Gerrard, 1989-1999. Mick has also written, co-written and edited many books and articles including: *Archaeology of Somerset*, with Ian Burrow, *Aspects of the Medieval Landscape of Somerset*, *Somerset from the Air* with Bob Croft, *Interpreting the Landscape from the Air*, *The Medieval Archaeology of Wessex* and *Archaeology is Rubbish - a beginner's guide* with Tony Robinson. Mick is an Emeritus Professor of Archaeology at Bristol University and Visiting Professor at Exeter and Durham Universities.

39 RURAL COMMENTATORS, ANTIQUARIANS AND GEOLOGISTS

William Marshall 1745–1818

AGRICULTURAL WRITER AND LAND AGENT / Visited Somerset in 1790s

William Marshall was the Yorkshire born son of a yeoman farmer and had a prodigious appetite for agricultural information. He started working in London in the linen trade, then went to the West Indies, working for an insurance agent. He came back and in 1774 started farming 300 acres at Addiscombe near Croydon. His partner went bankrupt and he found himself having to earn his living as a writer and land agent.

Marshall was a prolific writer and traveller. In 1787 he published the first of his major studies of the farming practices of five different regions of England: Norfolk, Yorkshire, Gloucestershire, the Midlands and in 1796 *The Rural Economy of the West of England* when he visited Somerset. Here he is talking about Taunton:

"The Market Place of Taunton is one of the first in the Kingdom; whether as to size, neatness, or accommodations: a triangular enclosure, fitted up with street of covered stalls, for butcher's meat, and furnished with spacious colonnades, for corn, poultry etc, and one for cheese, bacon, and other articles- which are sold, retail, by farmer's wives and daughters: an unusual but very political way of bringing these articles at once to the consumer; without the intervention of mere dealers."

John Billingsley 1747–1811

AGRICULTURAL PIONEER AND AUTHOR / Lived at Ashwick and Oakhill

John Billingsley was descended from a long line of gifted and talented dissenting Presbyterian ministers. His grandfather was minister of Ashwick from 1699 to 1729 and his great-grandfather, Nicholas Billingsley, was a noted poet, who died in Bristol in 1709. John Billingsley was born at Ashwick near Shepton Mallet but was not drawn to the cloth directly. In 1761 in the nearby village of Oakhill he founded the famous Oakhill Brewery which later made Oakhill Invalid Stout. The brewery finally closed in 2004. He also built his own house, Ashwick Grove.

In 1794 he published his *General View of the Agriculture of the County of Somerset* which is a masterly work encompassing a Survey of Somerset that gives the present-day historian much useful information. In 1798 he wrote about the water-meadows of the Brendon and Quantock Hills describing them as the best in the country. He was a great improver and is said to have 'drained Sedgemoor and enclosed Mendip'. Billingsley estimated that 13,600 acres of Mendip had been enclosed by dry stone walls. He also introduced the double-furrow plough. Billingsley was a founder member of the Bath and West Society and was involved with canal building and the turnpike trusts. He had an accurate view of the unenclosed way of agriculture and the efficiencies thus extolled…

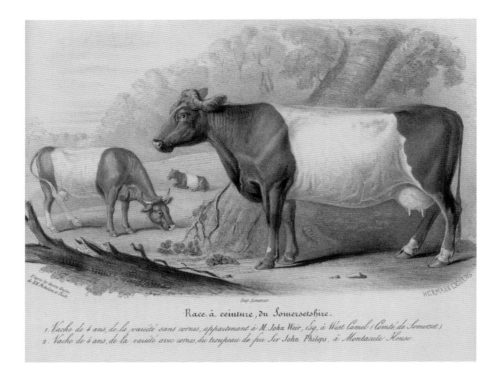

Race à ceinture, du Somersetshire.

1. Vache de 4 ans, de la variété sans cornes, appartenant à M. John Weir, Esq, à West Camel (Comté de Somerset)
2. Vache de 4 ans, de la variété avec cornes, du troupeau de feu Sir John Phileps, à Montacute House.

"The possession of a cow or two, with a hog, and a few geese, naturally exalts the peasant in his own conception above his brethren in the same rank of society. It inspires some degree of confidence in a property, inadequate to his support. In sauntering after his cattle, he acquires a habit of indolence. A quarter, half and occasionally whole days are imperceptibly lost…"

John Billingsey also recommends Taunton Vale Cider: 'It is supposed they possess an art peculiar to themselves, of conducting the fermentation and thereby preserving a rich and delicious flavour'. I suspect he is talking about keeving, a process which keeps the cider sweet by halting the first fermentation in its tracks and by continually racking the cider off the lees.

To see: Memorial to John Billingsley in Ashwick church.

John Collinson 1757–1793

ANTIQUARY / Vicar of Long Ashton

John Collinson was born in Wiltshire and went to Oxford. He published his first book, *The Beauties of British Antiquity* in 1779 and was ordained deacon the same year.

He served as a curate in various parishes including Marlborough and Cirencester, and became vicar of Clanfield in Oxfordshire. In 1784 Collinson was admitted a fellow of the Society of Antiquaries of London. In 1787 Collinson became vicar of Long Ashton and perpetual curate of Whitchurch (now absorbed into South Bristol). The first edition of his three volume *History & Antiquities of the County of Somerset, Collected from Authentick Records, and an Actual Survey made by the late Edmund Rack* was published in Bath in 1791. Edmund Rack had been secretary of the Agricultural and Philosophical Societies of Bath.

"Hemp, flax, teasels and woad are cultivated in considerable quantities. The plains are remarkable for their luxuriant herbage, particularly the moors on which are fattened great numbers of nearly the largest cattle in England. The sheep are generally of the smaller kind; the Mendip mutton is well known for its peculiar sweetness."

William Smith 1769-1839

GEOLOGIST / Lived south of Bath 1791-1799

Born in Oxfordshire, William Smith worked first in Gloucestershire as a surveyor and came to Somerset in 1791. He was employed on the Sutton Court Estate near the villages of Bishop Sutton and Stowey as a valuer. Later he worked for the Somerset Coal Company and was instrumental in the building of their canal. He worked for the canal engineer John Rennie and lived at various places: High Littleton, Tucking Mill, Midford, Dunkerton and Bath itself. It was at this time that he became fascinated by fossils and began to draw maps of soils and geological patterns. In 1799 he produced a geological map of the area around Bath. Until that point geological maps had always been in vertical section. His map, like the soils maps for the Agricultural Societies, was horizontal. This was a fundamental shift in alignment and proved much more useful to geologists and civil engineers. By 1815 he had created and published the first nationwide geological map upon which all other geological maps of Britain are based. He also published a book: *Delineation of the Strata of England and Wales.* Sadly his maps were often plagiarised and Smith went seriously into debt. He spent two years in the infamous King's Bench Prison in Southwark and was released in 1819. He then worked as an itinerant surveyor and helped build the Rotunda geological museum in Scarborough. It was not until 1831 that the Geological Society of London recognised William Smith's immense achievement and conferred on him the first ever Wollaston medal. It was on this occasion that the President referred to Smith as 'The Father of English Geology'. William Smith died in Northampton. Even a crater on Mars has been named after him.

John Rutter 1796-1851

TOPOGRAPHER AND POLITICAL AGENT / Born in Bristol

John Rutter was brought up as a Quaker and apprenticed to a linen draper in Shaftesbury. He later set up as a printer and was very much a self made man. He became friendly with William Beckford (see page 38) and in 1822 published *Delineations of Fonthill Abbey* followed by *An Historical and Descriptive Sketch of Wardour Castle and Demesne.* In 1829 he wrote *Delineations of Northwestern Somerset.* A very detailed and closely observed book. Some sections appeared as guides to Weston-super-Mare, Clevedon, and the Banwell bone caverns.

40 MODERN DAY SOMERSET HISTORIANS

Robert Dunning 1938–

COUNTY HISTORIAN / Lives in Taunton

Robert Dunning was born in East Coker but brought up at Clifton Maybank, near Yeovil. He was the County Historian for Somerset 1967–2005 and has written many fine books on the various aspects of Somerset's history. Robert went to university in Bristol and began work on the *Victoria County History of Somerset* in 1967 when Somerset County Council hired him to make a very detailed study of the county. The project, named the Victoria County Histories, was originally launched to celebrate the Queen Victoria's Diamond Jubilee. One of the first people to help the research on Somerset was Gladys Bradford of Thorney, educated at Cambridge University. Her grandson is Julian Temperley, the cider maker.

In his line of duty Robert Dunning spent perhaps 50,000 hours on research, visited some 380 churches and chapels and inspected 200 stately homes. The history was planned to run to 22 volumes. Nine have been published so far. He was ably assisted by Robin Bush and Mary Siraut; the latter now continues the work.

Robert's other books include: *A History of Somerset*, *A History of Christianity in Somerset*, *Wells Cathedral*, *Bridgwater*, *The Monmouth Rebellion*, *Somerset Churches*, *Somerset Monasteries*, *Arthur, King in the West*, and *Bath and Wells: a diocesan celebration*. Robert Dunning is a Fellow of the Society of Antiquaries of London and of the Royal Historical Society. He was appointed a Deputy Lieutenant for Somerset in 2007.

Robin Bush 1943–

COUNTY ARCHIVIST / Lives in Taunton

Born in Middlesex, Robin Bush read history at Exeter College, Oxford and in 1967 came to work in the Somerset Record Office as a historian and archivist until he retired in 1993. Robin has written many books about Somerset including *Somerset The Complete Guide*, *Somerset A Portrait in Colour* with Julian Comrie, *Somerset Stories Life and Laughter in Old Somerset*, *Somerset Bedside Book* a collection of prose and poetry, *The Book of Taunton* and *Taunton Castle*. Robin Bush has also made a career for himself as a lively member of the Channel 4's *Time Team* archaeology programme. From 2001 to 2005 he was Chairman of Somerset County Council.

Tom Mayberry 1956–

HISTORIAN AND AUTHOR / Lives in Taunton

Tom Mayberry is the Somerset County Heritage Officer. He has written *Coleridge and Wordsworth in the West Country*, *Coleridge and Wordsworth: the Crucible of Friendship*, *The Vale of Taunton Past*, *The Archaeology of Somerset* with Chris Webster, *Somerset Archaeology and Natural History* as editor, *Somerset The Millenium Book* with Hilary Binding and *Somerset: the Golden Years*.

Hilary Binding 1938–

LOCAL HISTORIAN, EDUCATIONAL CONSULTANT AND WRITER / *Lives in Carhampton*

Hilary Binding has lived in Carhampton for over thirty years. Her mother's family comes from West Somerset and she is a teacher by profession. Hilary Binding is a past chairman of both the Somerset Archaeological and Natural History Society and the West Somerset Village History Society. She edited the *Exmoor Review* for many years and at present edits *Exmoor The Country Magazine*.

Hilary has written several books on Somerset topics which include *Minehead, A New History* (with Douglas Stevens), *Discovering Dunster, Exmoor Century* (with Brian Pearce and Steven Pugsley), *The Book of Carhampton and Blue Anchor, Somerset The Millennium Book* (with Tom Mayberry), *Somerset Privies, Old Dulverton* (with Victor Bonham Carter) and *Somerset Cider: the Complete Story* (with Philippa Legg). *Big Drips from Bath and Wells* is a book for children commemorating the 1100th anniversary of the diocese of Bath and Wells. Hilary also writes a weekly column for the *West Somerset Free Press* and a collection of these writings has been published as *Exmoor By The Way*.

Christopher Culpin 1944–

HISTORIAN AND AUTHOR / *Lives in Castle Cary*

Christopher Culpin went to Cambridge University and has taught history all his life. He is passionate about the subject and has lived in Somerset since 1987. He has written a very wide variety of books, textbooks and teacher guides for secondary schools and National Trust properties as well as for BBC Schools TV programmes, online resources for the Wellcome Library and The

Science Museum. His books include: *Making History, Making Modern Britain, Past into Present, Medieval Realms, Making of the UK, Expansion Trade & Industry, The People's Century, Crime & Punishment, Modern History Study Guide, South Africa since 1948, The Norman Conquest, The Twentieth Century, Essential Germany 1918-45, SHP History Year 8*. He has also edited and contributed to many other books and has helped to formulate history as a subject for the National Curriculum.

42 THE ABODE OF LOVE — SPAXTON

THE ABODE OF LOVE was the name of the house of a religious community called Agapemone that lived in the village of Spaxton. It was a large house with its own grounds. It had eighteen bedrooms, servants' quarters, outhouses, stables, conservatories, gazebos and a series of garden cottages - as well as its own chapel furnished with easy chairs, settees and a billiard table. It was started by a defrocked clergyman called Henry James Prince who had been curate of Charlinch. He believed that the Holy Ghost had taken up residence in his body and directed his every action…

Prince had a faithful following of young wealthy women, both married and unmarried. He was often given to taking 'soul brides.' These included the five Nottidge sisters who each had £6000 settled on them after their father's death. Marriages were conveniently arranged for them and their money was used to pay the builders' bills. Sexual scandal and illegitimate children followed. The most notorious event was the Great Manifestation in 1856 when Prince deflowered a sixteen year old girl called Zoe Patterson on a couch in front of the altar, some say the billiard table, during a church service with hymns being sung and the organ going full pelt. He had chosen her from a group of twelve young girls all dressed in white. The congregation apparently took it in their stride, though one or two did try to leave. Prince died in 1899, much to the consternation of the community who thought he was immortal. His successor - Rev John Hugh Smyth-Pigott - claimed to be the reincarnation of Jesus Christ. The Agapemone community lasted till the 1950s and the property was sold off in 1958. The Abode of Love house is next to the Lamb Inn, Spaxton. Several books have been written on the Abode of Love. Prince wrote his own called *The Little Book Open*.

William Hepworth Dixon 1821-1879

A journalist and historian, Dixon visited Spaxton in 1867 and was able to interview Prince and had access to the community. He published his findings in a book called *Spiritual Wives* published in 1868. He also wrote *John Howard and the Prison World of Europe* and books about Admiral Blake and Lord Bacon. For a while Dixon was editor of *The Athenaeum* and also wrote travel books, including ones on the Holy Land, America, Russia and Cyprus as well as historical works on Catherine of Aragon and Anne Boleyn.

Other authors have written about the religious community at Spaxton:

Aubrey Menen *The Abode of Love* 1956

Donald McCormick *Temple of Love* 1962

Charles Mander: *The Reverend Prince and his Abode of Love* 1976

Kate Barlow: *The Abode of Love – A memoir* 2006

The Agapemone, Spaxton.

43 FROM PLUTARCH TO DEAD CATS – SOMERSET MISCELLANY 1

John Langhorne 1735-1779

POET AND TRANSLATOR / Lived in Blagdon, died in Blagdon

Born in Westmorland John Langhorne worked as a tutor in Yorkshire and wrote over 300 reviews for *Griffiths' Grand Magazine*. He went to Cambridge and ended up as a curate at Dagenham, Clerkenwell and then as an assistant preacher at Lincoln's Inn. He became rector of Blagdon in 1766. Sadly his first wife Ann died in childbirth. Their correspondence was published as *Letters to Eleonora*. Langhorne then went to live with his brother in Folkestone. In 1770 he translated *Plutarch's Lives* with critical notes and a new life of Plutarch in six volumes. It is for these works that he is chiefly remembered. His works of poetry include *Studley Park*, *Fables of Flora* and *Country Justice*. He married a second time and went on a tour of France and Flanders, returning to live at Blagdon, where he was made a Justice of the Peace. Sadly his second wife also died in childbirth. Langhorne was made a prebendary of Wells Cathedral. He took to drink and died at Blagdon House of 'rather too frequent draughts of Burton Ale.' He is buried in Blagdon.

Alfred Perceval Graves 1846-1931

POET AND EDUCATIONALIST / Lived in Taunton

Born in Dublin and a friend of Tennyson's, Alfred Perceval Graves worked as an Inspector of Schools and was the father of Robert Graves, the First World War poet. As a young man Alfred had worked as a poet and journalist, contributing to *Punch*, *The Gentleman's Magazine* and the *Spectator*. Alfred moved to Taunton from Yorkshire with his family in 1882 and was responsible for overseeing schools in West Somerset. But his real work was with Irish folk songs. In collaboration with Charles Stanford he published *Songs of Old Ireland*, as well as the famous *Ballad of Father O'Flynn*. He also published *Irish Songs and Ballads*. Airs from his *Irish Folk Songs* were arranged by Charles Wood and he worked with Wood on *Songs of Erin*. In 1891 he married Amy von Ranke whose father was Professor of Paediatrics at Munich University. Two years later he left Taunton and moved to Wimbledon where Robert Graves was born in 1895. In 1930 he published an autobiography called *To Return to All That*.

Horace Annesley Vachell 1861-1955

NOVELIST AND PLAYWRIGHT / Lived at Widcombe, Bath

Horace Vachell was born in Kent and served in the Rifle Brigade. He spent time in California and returned to England in 1900. He wrote more than fifty novels, including *John Charity*, *Brothers*, *The Hill*, *Her Son*, *The Fourth Dimension*, *The Fifth Commandment* and *Vicar's Walk* which was published in 1933 and describes life in Wells. He also wrote fifteen plays including *Quinney's* and *The Case of Lady Camber* and many short stories. He lived at Widcombe Manor.

New Pier, Weston-Super-Mare

45 FROM WESTON BACK TO WESTON: SOMERSET MISCELLANY 2

THIS SECTION is based on a wonderfully informative list of literary snippets and detailed research very kindly supplied by Christopher Richards of North Somerset Museum Service, Weston-super-Mare. There are some real gems in here…

John Oldmixon 1673-1742

HISTORIAN / Born near Weston-super-Mare

John Oldmixon was born at Oldmixon Manor near Weston-super-Mare. John's father (also John) died in 1675 and his mother in 1689 when John was 16 years old. John showed a talent for writing at an early age, went to London and was known to Pope, Addison and Steele. In 1708 he wrote *The British Empire in America*, followed by *The Secret History of Europe* and *Arcana Gallica, or the Secret History of France for the last Century*. As a source of income Oldmixon was offered the post of Collector at the Port of Bridgwater. An important job as Bridgwater was a thriving port in those days. He was often in trouble with the local authorities and frequented 'the Presbyterian and Baptist conventicles' and knew the names of people taking part in political demonstrations that paraded the streets. He was a vitriolic pamphleteer, wrote poetry and plays. Purcell composed the music for his opera called *Love's Paradise* which was performed at Drury Lane in 1700. His most successful play *The Governor of Cyprus* was performed, also at Drury Lane, in 1703. In 1730 he wrote a voluminous *History of England during the Reigns of the Royal House of Stuart*. His ballad *The Catholic Priest*, an attack on Pope's *Homer*, brought forth a retaliatory comment in Pope's *Dunciad*. Crippled with debt, gout and blindness Oldmixon died in 1742 and is supposed to have been buried at Ealing.

Hester Thrale alias Mrs Piozzi 1741-1821

DIARIST AND AUTHOR / Lived in Weston-super-Mare

Guidebooks and histories of Weston convey an impression of its early days as a seaside resort by quoting from a letter written by a Mrs Thrale Piozzi identified merely as 'a friend of Dr Johnson'. Mrs Piozzi was born in Caernarvonshire as Hester Lynch Salusbury and married Henry Thrale, a prosperous brewer of Southwark. They met Dr Johnson in 1765 and he became a member of their household. Johnson attracted so many leading figures of the day that Thrale's country house at Streatham became one of the cultural centres of England. Henry Thrale died in 1781 and Mrs Thrale married in 1784 the Italian musician Gabriel Piozzi. By this time, a literary career, she had embarked upon, was flourishing and several published works bear her name. Gabriel died in 1809 and his widow settled in Bath in 1814. Like many of her class, she came to Weston to breathe sea-air and bathe in sea-water, aids to good health. On the 27th August 1819 she wrote the letter, so often quoted in Weston guidebooks and histories, that describes the place as 'neither gay nor fashionable, yet as full as an egg' and with only two books, a Bible and a *Paradise Lost*! Mrs Piozzi had been a daring horsewoman and had shown an almost masculine courage and energy throughout her life so it is no surprise to read in another of her Weston letters: 'My fearlessness in the water attracts the women to the rocks, where it seems such fine sport to see Mrs Piozzi'. She was in her late seventies at this time. The rocks were those at Anchor Head, traditionally a ladies bathing place. At the time of her visit to Weston she was infatuated with William Augustus Conway a stage actor nearly 50 years her junior. There are tales of an offer of marriage and of gifts to Conway from Mrs Piozzi. Her love letters to him were published in 1843 but doubts have been cast on their authenticity. See also Hester Thrale, page 44.

Anna Sawyer

POET / Lived in Rowberrow c. 1795

Anna Sawyer flourished between 1794 to 1801. She was born near Rowberrow according to *Poems on Various Subjects* (Birmingham 1801) and was known to T. S. Whalley and Hannah More. Anna was the wife of William Sawyer of Bristol who died in Birmingham on 23 May 1808. Her husband may well have had a connection with calamine-mining at Rowberrow. Her poems include *Lines, Written On Seeing My Husband's Picture, Painted When Young, Cheddar, Lines, Written near Rowberrow, in Somersetshire, where the Author lately resided, Glasbury Abbey. An Address to Millers, Badgers, and the whole Fraternity of Dealers in Corn and Flour, as well as Sunday Schools, On the Present Fashionable Female Dresses* and *Elegy on Mortality*. In apologizing to subscribers for the smallness of the work the editor blames the 'unexpected duty on paper', which caused the author to restrict her original design. Hannah More bought two copies. Mr and Mrs Sawyer ran a school and her list of subscribers to her privately printed poems is impressive. It includes Matthew Boulton the industrialist and engineer who was a partner of James Watt. They made Boulton and Watt steam engines.

Ianthe Shelley 1813–1876

Shelley's daughter, Ianthe, 1813-76 is buried under a beech tree in Cothelstone churchyard on the Quantocks. Her mother Harriet, unfortunately drowned herself in the Serpentine in 1816. Ianthe wisely married Edward Edward Jeffries Esdaile whose family had acquired the Cothelstone manor and estates in 1793.

Wilkie Collins 1824–1889

NOVELIST / Visited Weston-super-Mare 1855

In *The Moonstone* by Wilkie Collins, Gustavus St Brody, a French botanist is cast as 'the science teacher'. Brody lived in Weston-super-Mare in 1855 at the time of Wilkie Collins' visit to the seaside resort to which he refers in *The Cruise of the Tom Tit*. Brody lectured in Weston and wrote the first *Flora* of the town. Col. Rogers of Uphill House, south of Weston, had a daughter Mary who married Count Giovanni Possente. He is cast as 'Count P.' in *The Moonstone*. The most quoted source for a part of the story comes from a real event in Somerset in 1860, the notorious Road Hill murder case, where a four year old boy was murdered by his half sister in the small Somerset village of Rode near Frome. See also *The Suspicions of Mr Whicher: or the Murder at Road Hill House* by Kate Summerscale. Somerset is used as a location in another Wilkie Collins novel called *Armadale*.

Morton Luce 1848-1943

WRITER AND CRITIC / Lived in Weston-super-Mare

Morton Luce was a man of letters and for many years editor of the Arden Shakespeare plays and an expert on Shakespeare's sonnets. He wrote a handbook to Tennyson and his poems. Luce also knew Mary and Henry Webb and dedicated two sonnets to Mary Webb. He intended to publish a work entitled *The Real Mary Webb*.

Frank Castle Froest 1858-1930

POLICEMAN AND CRIME WRITER / Born in Bristol · Died in Weston-super-Mare

Froest was Detective Superintendent of Scotland Yard and a crime-fighter of legendary stature. He retired to Weston-super-Mare and wrote crime novels. *The Grell Mystery* (1913), *The Crime Club* (1915), and *The Rogues' Syndicate* (1916). Two of his novels, *The Grell Mystery* and *The Maelstrom*, were made into films in 1917.

Baroness Orczy 1866–1947

Born in Hungary, her father was a composer and her mother a countess. She was a prolific novelist and her best known works are the Scarlet Pimpernel stories. She also wrote short detective stories and part of *Lady Molly of Scotland Yard* is set around Weston-super-Mare.

Ernest Bramah Smith 1868–1942

NOVELIST AND SHORT STORY WRITER / Died in Weston-super-Mare

Known as Ernest Bramah he was secretary to Jerome K. Jerome. Bramah was a recluse and lived at number 40 Boulevard in Weston-super-Mare where he died. He was a novelist and short story writer. Bramah created the characters Kai Lung and Max Carrados. George Orwell acknowledged that Bramah's book *What Might Have Been* influenced his own *Nineteen Eighty-Four*. Bramah has been credited with the invention of the saying, widely quoted as an ancient Chinese curse, "May you live in interesting times".

Hilaire Belloc 1870–1953

He came to lecture to Weston-super-Mare and at another time was involved in a road accident at Farrington Gurney. At his funeral Mass, Monsignor Ronald Knox observed, "No man of his time fought so hard for the good things."

G. K. Chesterton 1874–1936

There is a reference to a 'Mendip Mine' in his poem *Wine and Water* and other references to Somerset in his works. G.K. Chesterton was of large stature and girth. On another occasion he remarked to his friend George

Sunshine in the Gorge

Bernard Shaw 'To look at you, anyone would think there was a famine in England.' Shaw retorted, 'To look at you, anyone would think you caused it.'

Dolf Wyllarde 1871-1950

Lived at Oldmixon Manor near Weston-super-Mare. Dolf Wyllarde was a novelist of national fame who published forty one books. She travelled widely. The manor was full of books and ornaments that she had brought home from overseas. Her effects were auctioned off in 1950 when John Bailey visited the house. Then it was ivy clad and inside dull and Victorian. In the stables were her 1927 Humber and her 1929 Morris and a splendidly preserved trap with gleaming coachwork and carriage lamps. In the stables was a tablet that read: 'In memory of Sappho, a Gallant Horse and a Great Lady, 1911-1934'. Beneath a tree in the grounds is a memorial to a cat that the narrator named Felise in a Wyllarde novel given that name. The stone reads 'Fluffles. Original of Felise. Dolf Wyllarde's Cat, 1923-1934'. She was educated at Kings College, London and was a journalist before writing novels. She lived as a recluse.

Naomi Royde-Smith 1875-1964 *Wells*

Literary editor and novelist who lived in Wells during the 1930s. Her novel *Urchin Moor* (1939) is set around Clevedon.

Dion Fortune 1890-1946

NOVELIST AND OCCULT WRITER / Lived in Highbridge and Glastonbury

Brought up in Wales, Dion reported seeing visions of Atlantis at age four. She lived at Highbridge and went to school in Weston-super-Mare. Her books include *The Demon Lover*, *The Winged Bull*, *The Goat-Foot God*, and *The Secrets of Dr. Taverner*, as well as *The Sea Priestess* which is based on Brean Down and *Moon Magic*. She also wrote *The Cosmic Doctrine*, *The Mystical Qabalah* and *Psychic Self-Defense*. She then moved to Glastonbury where she is still revered by the New Age fraternity.

Cecil Day-Lewis 1904-1972

The Poem *Seen from a Train* (1948) was written between Yeovil and Crewkerne.

W. H. Auden 1907-1973

POET / Visited Mendip in 1970

Auden stayed with Anthony Rossiter of Chewton Mendip. He visited Wells and also stayed in Cothay Manor near Wellington. Auden had a passion for limestone.

Antony Rossiter 1926-2001

Educated at Eton and Chelsea Art School, Rossiter taught at Millfield from 1955 onwards. From 1983 he was a lecturer at the Royal West of England Academy in Bristol. He stayed with Robert Frost who encouraged him to write *The Pendulum*, an autobiography referring to mental illness.

M. M. Kaye 1908–2004

NOVELIST / Educated in Clevedon

Born in India, Mary Margaret Kaye was educated at a boarding school called The Lawn in Clevedon. She writes about these years in her autobiography *Share of Summer*. Kaye is best known for her novel *The Far Pavilions* which was filmed in 1984. She also wrote *Shadow of the Moon*, *Trade Wind* and many detective novels such as *Death in Kashmir*, *Death in Zanzibar*, *Death in Cyprus* and *Death in Berlin*. She also wrote six children's stories.

Victor Canning 1911–1986

NOVELIST AND CRIME WRITER / Lived in Weston–super–Mare

Born in Plymouth, Victor Canning was well known as a crime writer. In 1934, his first novel. *Mr. Finchley Discovers his England*, became a runaway best seller. It was written whilst he was living in Weston-super- Mare. In 1935 he married Phyllis McEwen, a girl from a theatrical family who was working with a touring vaudeville production at Weston. This was followed by *Mr. Finchley Goes to Paris* in 1938 and *Mr. Finchley Takes the Road* in 1940. During the war he joined up with the novelist and spy writer, Eric Ambler. Canning then served in North Africa, Sicily and Italy. After the war he wrote many crime novels including *The Chasm*, *Panther's Moon*, *The Golden Salamander*, *The Whip Hand*, the first of his Rex Carver books, *Firecrest* and *The Rainbird Pattern*. He also wrote children's books and an *Arthurian trilogy: The Crimson Chalice, The Circle of the Gods, The Immortal Wound.*

Henry de Vere Stacpoole 1863–1951

NOVELIST AND DOCTOR / Lived in the Pensford area 1898

Born in Dublin, Harry Stacpoole is best known for his work *Blue Lagoon* which has been filmed several times. He was a ship's doctor for many years and started out on a cable mending vessel. This enabled him to have time to write. Stacpoole was also an expert on the South Pacific islands. Occasionally he came back to England and in the summer of 1898 Stacpoole practised as a country doctor in Somerset. Here in 1899 he wrote his own favourite among his books, *The Doctor: A Study from Life*, set in the Pensford coal-mining area: a story of English village life centering upon an old doctor and a French niece who comes to upset his routine. To Stacpoole's disappointment this book also failed to impress the public. It was his fifth novel. He also lived in Bath. Success came with *Blue Lagoon* in 1908 which was reprinted at least twenty-four times in thirteen years. He also wrote poetry, including translations of Sappho and François Villon. In all Stacpoole, wrote more than sixty books. He also wrote under the pseudonym Tyler De Saix.

F. N. Butterworth c.1865–1952

NOVELIST /Lived in Weston–super–Mare

F.N. Butterworth died in Weston-super-Mare in 1952. He went to sea in 1885 as a Marine Engineer and then lived in Borneo for 12 years and became a friend of the Sultan of Brunei. His experiences there gave him the material he needed for his novels, which were praised by both H.G. Wells and George Orwell. Under the pen-name Peter Blundell he wrote *Mr Podd of Borneo*, *Princess of the Yellow Moon*, *Oh, Mr Bidgood*, *The Sins of Neil Godfrey* and *Morals of Matilda*. He came back to England in 1913 and from 1914-18 worked at Woolwich Arsenal.

GRAND PIER, WESTON-SUPER-MARE.

46 GUIDEBOOKS AND LOCAL HISTORY: SOMERSET MISCELLANY 3

T HIS IS A SLIGHTLY RANDOM but delightful series of titles that highlight the diversity and oddity of Somerset's landscape and local history: *so wet and weely, so miry and moorish*, as William Camden would say.

Joseph Henry Wade

Born in 1861, he lived on Worlebury Hill, near Weston-super-Mare. In 1907 he wrote *A Little Guide to Somerset* with his brother George Woosung Wade. Their father owned a barque called the *Enterprise* and often sailed to China. Wade also wrote *The Dowser: A Story of A Mendip Mystery, Isle of Ill Repute* and several rambling guides: *Glamorgan, Rambles in Cathedral Cities, Rambles in Cornwall* and *Rambles in Shakespeare Country*.

Ann Garnett

Caught from Time and Fields of Young Corn. Country diaries from the Brendons and Quantocks in the 1920s.

Stuart Mais

A popular writer and broadcaster between the wars: *Walking in Somerset*. A cut above the usual guidebooks of this period.

Sylvia Townsend Warner

Somerset 1949. A delightful and closely observed guide.

Monica Hutchings

Mendip and Avalon, Inside Somerset, Brief guide to Somerset, Rural Reflections, Chronicles of Church Farm. The Blue Island, Green Willow, Romany Cottage and *Hardy's River.*

Shirley Toulson

Mendip Hills – the threatened Landscape, Blackdown Hills of Somerset and Devon, Somerset with Bristol and Bath, The Celtic year, The Companion Guide to Devon, The Drovers Roads of Wales with Fay Godwin, and *Drovers Roads of South Wales*. She has also written four collections of poems.

Edward Hutton

Highways and Byways of Somerset. Many books on various aspects of Somerset including *The Somerset & Dorset Railway, Old Mendip, North Somerset's Gunpowder Mills* and *Mendip – a New Study*.

Bel Mooney

Bel Mooney's Somerset 1985

Desmond Hawkins

Wessex, A Literary Celebration 1991

Janet White

Sheepstell: autobiography of a shepherd 1991

Rodney Legg

Steep Holm Legends, Steep Holm Allsop Island, The Steep Holm Guide. Exmoor walks

Diana Crighton

Time for Somerset 2006

Lionel Ward

Taunton A–Z 2008

Kate Lynch

Willow 2003
Sheep from Lamb to Loom 2009

47 BOOKS ABOUT THE SOMERSET LEVELS AND MOORS

Michael Williams *Draining of the Somerset Levels* 1970

Bernard Storer *Natural History of the Somerset Levels* 1972

Adam Nicholson *Wetland Life in the Somerset Levels* photography Patrick Sutherland 1986

Desmond Hawkins *Avalon and Sedgemoor* 1982

Chris Chapman *Secrets of the Moor* 1992, *Secrets of the Levels* 1996

Robin and Romey Williams *The Somerset Levels* 1992

Chris Willoughby *Somerset* 1993

James Crowden

In Time of Flood photography George Wright 1996 *Bridgwater – the Parrett's Mouth*, photography Pauline Rook 2000. *Working Women of Somerset*, photography Pauline Rook 2001

Hard at it...catching eels   *James Crowden and Andrew Crane*

Nancy Ashworth *Voices from the Peat* 2004

Tony Anderson *Life on the Levels* photography Chris Willoughby 2006

Dudley Doust *Bradley Brook – An American Walks Down an English River* 2009

James Lynch *Skylines – Visionary Paintings of Wessex* 2006 with poems by David Caddy, James Crowden and Mary Maher

48 FROM PSYCHOLOGY TO CIDER – SOMERSET MISCELLANY 4

Richard Gregory 1923–

EXPERIMENTAL PSYCHOLOGIST AND AUTHOR / Lives in Clifton

Born in London, Richard Gregory served in the RAF for five years specialising in signals and radar. In 1947 he went to Cambridge where he read Philosophy and Experimental Psychology. He worked for the Royal Navy on submarine escape and then went back to Cambridge where he became a lecturer in the Department of Experimental Psychology, specialising in perception, scientific method and cybernetics. He became a fellow of Corpus Christi College and then taught in America. In 1966 he published *Eye and Brain* followed by *The Intelligent Eye*. He then worked on artificial intelligence in Edinburgh. In 1970 he was appointed Professor of Neuro-psychology and Director of the Brain and Perception Laboratory at the Medical School at Bristol University.

Whilst there he wrote *The Oxford Companion to the Mind* and *Mind in Science*. Richard is a great man for exhibitions. He set up *Illusion in Nature and Art* with Sir Roland Penrose and Sir Ernst Gombrich, as well as the Bristol Exploratory that over 12 years attracted over two Million paying visitors. His other books include *Even Odder Perceptions* and *Mirrors in the Mind*.

Dr John Hurrell Crook 1930–

EVOLUTIONARY PSYCHOLOGIST, AUTHOR AND BUDDHIST TEACHER / Lives near Shipham

John Crook was born in Southampton; gained his degree at Southampton University in zoology and his PhD in animal behaviour at Cambridge. He served in the army in Hong Kong during the Korean War with an anti aircraft regiment. It was here that in Hong Kong that he first became interested in Zen Buddhism. For many years

Famous for dependability, because of consistent high quality materials and workmanship allied to excellence of design, AUSTIN cars have earned the confidence of Motorists everywhere.

The Car illustrated is the

'AUSTIN TEN'
CAMBRIDGE SALOON
£178

HENLYS
CHELTENHAM RD., BRISTOL

John was a Reader in Ethology in the Psychology Department at Bristol University studying the evolution of social organization of birds and mammals. Some of his original work was with African weaver birds; later he researched gelada baboons in Ethiopia. In India he also worked with Dr Salim Ali of the Bombay Natural History Society. John Crook has led many expeditions as well as an internationally known research group from Bristol for which he was awarded a DSc. Subsequently John moved into social anthropology studying village and monastic organisation in Ladakh in the Western Himalaya. John has a serious interest in Buddhism and has trained with many Chan, Zen and Tibetan Buddhist teachers. He has created an educational Buddhist charity called The Western Chan Fellowship, after receiving transmission to teach from Ven Master Shen Yeng of Dharma Drum Mountain, Taiwan. John has written many books including *The Evolution of Human Consciousness*; *Himalayan Buddhist Villages: Environment, Resources, Society and Religious Life in Zangskar, Ladakh* with Henry Osmaston; *The Yogins of Ladakh: A Pilgrimage Among the Hermits of the Buddhist Himalayas* with James Lowe and *Illuminating Silence: edited talks of Master Shen Yeng*; *Koans of Layman John*. His latest book *World Crisis and Buddhist Humanism. End Games: Collapse or Renewal of Civilisation* was published in 2009.

John Polkinghorne 1930–

Scientist, theologian and author / Born in Weston-super-Mare

John Polkinghorne started his education in Street and then went to Cambridge and read mathematics. His real interest was in particle physics;·he was Professor of Mathematical Physics at Cambridge from 1968 to 1979. He was then ordained as an Anglican priest in 1982 and he served as a curate of a large working-class parish in Bristol. He then became very interested in the interface between religion and science. He has sat on the Medical Ethics Committee of the BMA for many years.

John Polkinghorne has written many science books and papers, including *The Analytic S-Matrix*, *The Particle Play*, *Models of High Energy Processes*, *The Quantum World* and *Quantum Theory: A Very Short Introduction*. His many books on Christianity and science include *The Way the World is*, *Quarks, Chaos and Christianity*, *Scientists as Theologians*, *Quantum Physics and Theology: An Unexpected Kinship* and *From Physicist to Priest, an Autobiography*.

John Polkinghorne considers that "the question of the existence of God is the single most important question we face about the nature of reality."

Henry Hobhouse 1924–

Author and journalist / Lives in Woolavington

Henry Hobhouse has been a journalist for *The Economist*, *New Chronicle*, *Daily Express* and the *Wall Street Journal*.

In 1985 he published *Seeds of Change: Five Plants That Transformed Mankind* which gives insights into the trading and political history of quinine, sugar, tea, cotton and the potato. In the second edition coca was added as a sixth plant. His second book, *Forces of Change: An Unorthodox View of History* looked at global population dynamics. His third, *Seeds of Wealth*, dealt with commodities that enriched men: timber, wine, rubber and tobacco.

Penelope Hobhouse 1929–

Garden writer / Lives at Hadspen, near Castle Cary

Born in Northern Ireland, Penelope Hobhouse is a garden writer, designer and lecturer. She read economics at Cambridge and then went walking in Tuscany. She married and went to live at Hadspen House near Castle Cary, where she restored the gardens. She was later in charge of the gardens at Tintinhull House. She started writing and presented programmes on television. Her books include: *Colour in Your Garden*, *Plants in Garden History*, *Gardens of Italy*, *A Garden Journal*, *Penelope Hobhouse on Gardening*, *Penelope Hobhouse's Garden Designs* and *Penelope Hobhouse's Natural Planting*. She has designed gardens in England, Scotland, France, Italy, Spain, Germany and the United States. She has received many awards including the Royal Horticultural Society Victoria Medal of Honour and the Life Time Achievement Award from the Guild of Garden Writers.

For a while she lived at Bettiscombe in Dorset but in 2008 she moved back to Hadspen, where she is starting a new garden.

Don McCullin 1935–

PHOTOGRAPHER AND AUTHOR / Lives near Bruton

Don McCullin was born in London and served in the RAF on National Service during the Suez crisis in 1956, as a photographer's assistant. His work for the *Sunday Times* from 1966 to 1984 resulted in a role as their star photographer; since 1985 he has been a freelance photojournalist. For the last 40 years, he has covered almost every war there is, except the Falklands in 1982, when the British Government refused to grant him a press pass. His shots of Cyprus, Beirut, Vietnam, Biafra, Northern Ireland, Cambodia and El Salvador are monumental and haunting, providing some of the most potent visual images of the 20th century. The level of suffering witnessed during these conflicts has had a profound influence on his life. His photographs are in a sense wordless essays in themselves, evoking powerful feelings and reactions. In a search for peace, McCullin has also turned his lens on the Somerset landscape and on still life compositions. *Open Skies* has an introduction by John Fowles. He has produced many books, including an autobiography *Unreasonable Behaviour*, *Sleeping with Ghosts*, *The Homecoming*, a look at depression in the north of England around Consett, *The Palestinians* with Jonathan Dimbleby, *Beirut: A City in Crisis* and *Don McCullin in Africa*. He has had major retrospective exhibitions and his pictures form part of permanent national collections in England and the United States. He has won many awards for his work and was made a CBE in 1993, the first photojournalist to receive such an honour. In 2006 McCullin was awarded the Cornell Capa Award.

This business of farming

Food production is news these days, and the farm is becoming ever more highly organised towards a greater efficiency and a more effective economy. Much has already been done—and the results are nowhere more noticeable than in the farmer's 'office', where problems of business rather than of agriculture are taking up an increasing amount of his time. To assist him with these problems the wise farmer makes full use of the banking facilities placed at his disposal by the Westminster Bank, secure in the knowledge that the Bank's service to farmers is based upon long practical experience and a deep understanding of their needs.

W E S T M I N S T E R   B A N K   L I M I T E D

Quentin Seddon 1941–

JOURNALIST AND AUTHOR / Lives near Bruton

Quentin Seddon moved to Somerset in 1987 and manages an extensive small holding. He describes himself as a 'gentleman peasant.' He has presented many radio and television farming programmes and has written for *The Guardian*, *Country Living* and *Resurgence*. He has written several books including *A Brief History of Thyme: From Magical Powers to the Elixir of Youth* and *The Silent Revolution*.

Liz Copas 1942–

POMOLOGIST AND AUTHOR / Lives near Crewkerne

Liz Copas is one of the last scientists to have worked at the famous Long Ashton Research Station outside Bristol. She is a pomologist and has been very influential in helping not only to identify apples, but to research lost varieties and to help with all aspects of orchard management. Her book *Somerset Pomona* is essential reading for all those interested in the history of Somerset's rich tradition of cider apple cultivation, and the making of cider itself.

food and cookery. These include: *Rhodes Around Britain, New British Classics, Complete Cookery Year, Keeping it Simple, Time to Eat* and *'Gary Rhodes: 365'*.

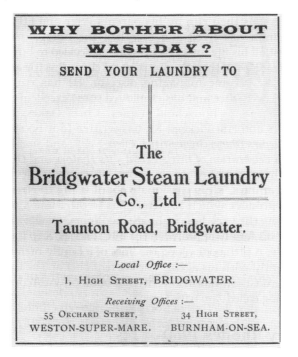

WHY BOTHER ABOUT WASHDAY?

SEND YOUR LAUNDRY TO

The
Bridgwater Steam Laundry
Co., Ltd.

Taunton Road, Bridgwater.

Local Office :—
1, HIGH STREET, BRIDGWATER.

Receiving Offices :—
55 ORCHARD STREET,   34 HIGH STREET,
WESTON-SUPER-MARE.   BURNHAM-ON-SEA.

Tamasin Day-Lewis 1953–

FOOD WRITER AND JOURNALIST / Lives near Bridgwater

Tamasin Day-Lewis is the daughter of the poet Cecil Day-Lewis and brother of Daniel Day-Lewis. She went to Cambridge and read English at King's College. She writes for *The Daily Telegraph*, *Vanity Fair*, *Vogue* and *Food Illustrated*. Her many books include: *Last Letters Home;*

West of Ireland Summers: A Cookbook; The Art of the Tart ; Good Tempered Food: Recipes to Love, Leave and Linger Over; Simply the Best: The Art of Seasonal Cooking; Tarts with Tops on: Or How to Make the Perfect Pie; Tamasin's Kitchen Bible; Tamasin's Kitchen Classics and *Where Shall We Go For Dinner?: A Food Romance.* Her latest book is *Supper for a Song.* Tamasin has also carved out a career for herself as a television chef. Her daughter, Miranda Shearer, has also written two books *Cheap as Chips, Better than Toast; Easy Recipes for Students* and *Big Secrets for Not so Little Girls.*

Kevin McCloud 1958–

DESIGNER, AUTHOR AND TV PRESENTER / Lives near Frome

Born in Bedfordshire, Kevin studied History of Art and Architecture at Cambridge, and speaks French and Italian, attributes recently put to good use in his *Grand Tour* TV series, with accompanying book, encompassing European masterpieces known to have influenced subsequent generations. Originally a theatre and lighting designer, today he concentrates on TV work, product design, journalism and writing books, of which he has written many titles on design themes. He is best known for his work on the Channel 4 series *Grand Designs*, covering unusual building projects, seeing people's often impractical dreams through from drawing board to completion. Despite the contemporary angle of these programmes, he lives in a 15th century farmhouse in Somerset, where he enjoys the surrounding orchards and the fruits and cider thereof. He is patron of Somerset Arts, an Ambassador for WWF and involved with environmental projects, including his own company HAB (Happiness, Architecture, Beauty) which is committed to working with local communities, providing sustainable, affordable housing.

Carol Trewin 1953-2009

FOOD WRITER / Born and brought up in Bristol

Carol Trewin grew up in Clifton and went to Exeter University where she read English. She moved to Yorkshire, had a milk round, market garden, and ran a small shop. In 1986 she joined the BBC and moved from York to London where she worked for Radio 4 on Woman's Hour, The Food Programme and The World Service. She became editor of Farming Today and head of the BBC's Rural Affairs Department at Pebble Mill in Birmingham. On Your Farm was her best loved programme and in the four years she produced the programme, she recorded over 200 farm breakfasts. In 1997 she won a Sony award for her coverage of BSE with Apocalypse Cow. A year later when the BBC wanted to axe the farming programme she fought to save it. The only concession, the timing, which is now 5.45am.

Carol then worked as Farming Editor for the *Western Morning News*, covering the South West and in particular Foot and Mouth Disease. She then worked for Taste of the West in Cornwall and in 2004 returned to the *Western Morning News* and became the Food Editor, a job she relished. Carol also wrote three books: *Gourmet Cornwall*, *Cornish Fishing and Seafood* and *The Devon Food Book*; all illustrated by photographer Adam Woolfitt.

James Crowden 1954-

POET AND WRITER / Lives in Winsham

James Crowden was born in Plymouth and brought up on the western edge of Dartmoor. He joined the Army in 1972 and has travelled widely in the Middle East, Iran and Afghanistan. In 1976-77 he spent a winter in the Himalaya, trapped for six months in the Zangskar Valley in Ladakh. He studied civil engineering at Bristol and anthropology at Oxford. After a spell in the Outer Hebrides he worked in Bristol Docks as a boatman and in 1980 settled in Dorset. In 1986 he then migrated over the border into Somerset. He worked for twenty years as a casual agricultural labourer involved with cider making, night lambing, sheep shearing and forestry. His first book *Blood Earth and Medicine* came out in 1991. Other books include *In Time of Flood*, *Cider the Forgotten Miracle*, *Waterways*, *The Wheal of Hope*, *The Bad Winter*, *Dorset Man*, *Dorset Women*, *Dorset Coast* and *Dorset Footsteps*. In 2009 *Ciderland* won the prestigious André Simon Food and Drink Award.

Winter flooding on West Sedgemoor © Chris Chapman

INDEX OF WRITERS

ORCHIDS

Someone suddenly sang in the darkness
In the empty desert night;
He sang for company as he shovelled sand,
Digging himself a shelter for the night.
In the bare cold sand and singing of orchids.
And at once in the darkness I saw them,
Orchids,
Green and fungus- yellow and spotted ones
Fantastically winged and pouting,
Sticky-seeming like shapes of wax
With pouting pale antennae.

Are these flowers with the sticky waxen petals?
They are not appropriate in fields nor to memory,
But are held between the fingers of fat gentlemen
Or fixed in the hair of slim girls in ballrooms.
Even here in this desert where a flower would be wonder,
Even here I wish for none of them.

But I will remember purple orchids,
Early purple in the fields above Cheddar,
With spotted orchids among them:-
Small pointed trumpets on a tiny stem
(flowers fading to pink in the sun of Summer),
With the rusty-black spotted green leaves.
These are flowers for a song, grown of the fields,
These I will remember.

JOHN JARMAIN

This poem was written in the Western Desert just before
the Battle of El Alamein in October 1942. It was sent
back home in a letter by John Jarmain to his young
wife in Somerset, after the the end of the battle. The
letter is dated 9th November 1942.

INDEX OF PLACES

" 'E ain't zo savageous."

PICTURE ACKNOWLEDGEMENTS

The majority of the illustrations are from James Crowden's own collection, with the exception of the following, whom the publisher thanks for copyright permission:

Mark Adler/Mendip Times *174T, B, 175*

Ashmolean Museum, University of Oxford *8R*

Trustees of the British Museum/Dept of Prints & Drawings *189*

Chris Chapman © **www.chrischampanphotography.com** *112, 246*

Iain Claridge Studio *242*

Sir Ranulph Fiennes/ photo Ian Parnell **www.ianparnell.com** *144*

Jenny de Gex Collection *126, 150-151, 156, 167, 182, 185, 224, 227, 230, 233*

Glastonbury Antiquarian Society *203*

Gothic Image Publications, photo David Speed, from *New Light on the Ancient Mystery of Glastonbury*, 1990 *165R*

Guardian Newspapers *90*

Courtesy of the Estate of Clare Leighton *240, 241L, R, 254*

Kate Lynch © *235*

James Lynch © *237*

Maerton Stud, Spaxton *213*

Julia Manning © **www.juliamanning.net** *223*

Museo de Arte de Ponce, Puerto Rico *16*

National Portrait Gallery, London *46, 51, 73, 122*

National Portrait Gallery, London / © Mark Gerson *105*

National Trust, Lytes Cary Manor/Pauline Rook *20*

National Trust Photo Library, Clevedon Court/A.C. Cooper *70*

National Trust Photo Library, Clevedon Court/ John Hammond *179*

Orchardleigh House/ **www.orchardleigh.net** courtesy of St Mary's Church, Orchardleigh *120L*

Neil Phillips © **www.neilphillipsphotography.co.uk** *Front cover, 245*

The Powys Society **www.powys-society.org** *100, 101*

Project Gutenberg Literary Archive Foundation *173*

Quantock Towers Benefice/Church of the Holy Ghost, Crowcombe /JdeG *113*

The Quekett Microscopical Club © Tony Dutton, Collections Archivist and Curator *211L*

Pauline Rook © *54*

Somerset County Council Museum Service *256*

St Aldhelm's Church, Bishopstrow *8L*

St Michael's Church, East Coker *52*

St Peter & St Paul Church, Odcombe/Pauline Rook *21L*

The Victoria Art Gallery, Bath and North East Somerset Council *40*

Wells Literary Festival *94, 130, 140, 155L, 208*

Angela Willliams © *131*

The Woodforde Society/JdeG *152*

George Wright © *133,159*

Every effort has been made to trace the copyright holders. The Publisher apologises in advance for any unintentional omissions and would be prepared, if any such case should arise, to add the appropriate acknowledgement to any future edition of the book.

NOTES ON SOME ILLUSTRATIONS

16: *The Last Sleep of Arthur in Avalon* by Sir Edward Burne-Jones (1833-98). At over 9' high x 21' wide this was Burne-Jones final masterpiece, taking the last 20 years of his life. Burne-Jones designed many embroideries for Frances Horner of Mells, whose sons were killed in WWI. Her daughter married Raymond Asquith, son of the Prime Minister, also killed in WWI. One of those embroideries still hangs in Mells Church today.

40: *The Savile Map*, 1603, signed by Henry Savile, one of the earliest and most important maps of Bath, pre-dating Speed.

46: *William Dampier* by Thomas Murray.

51: Thomas Stearns (TS) Eliot by an unknown photographer.

70: *The Traveller's Breakfast* by Edward Villiers Rippingille, 1824. Shown in this fantasy tableau, which can be seen at Clevedon Court, are Samuel Taylor Coleridge, William and Dorothy Wordsworth, Robert Southey, Joseph Cottle et al, en route from Bristol to the Quantocks.

73: *Mary Wollstonecraft Shelley* by Richard Rothwell.

100: The Powys family: in the back row, from right to left, Theodore on far right with John Cowper next to him. Philippa is far left of middle row and Llewelyn far left of front row.

105: Evelyn Waugh with his family and two Italian servants.

122: Siegfried Sassoon photographed by Lady Ottoline Morrell.

179: *William Makepeace Thackeray* (1811-1863) drawing with colour wash by Sir Joseph Edgar Boehm, on the stairs and landing at the entrance to the Thackeray Room at Clevedon Court.

223: *Wotan's Wut, a discussion between ravens*. Limited edition etching by Julia Manning.

235: *John and Tony Richards with their Exmoor Horn rams, Porlock* by Kate Lynch, in *Sheep, From Lamb to Loom*, 2009.

237: *Burrow Mump from Turn Hill* by James Lynch, in *Skylines*, 2006.

BOOKS AND MAPS:

Antiquities, William Stukeley, 1724 *4-5, 6, 14*

Camden's Britannia, 1695 English edition, translated from the 1586 Latin edition by Edmund Gibson, with maps by Robert Morden *endpapers,12, 23, 55, 56-57, 96, 168*

Dampier's Voyages, William Dampier, 1906 edition, edited by John Masefield *47,48, 49, 50, 211R*

Micah Clarke, Arthur Conan Doyle, 1893, 12th edition *148, 149*

A Thousand Miles Up the Nile, 1877, engravings by G. Pearson after drawings by the author, Amelia Edwards *200, 201, 202*

Nature Caricatures, Sketches from Exmoor, Sir Francis Carruthers Gould, 1929 *vi, xvi, 109, 111, 214, 253*

Wells and Glastonbury, Thomas Scott Holmes, engravings by Edmund New, 1908 by courtesy of Pamela Egan *19, 76, 78, 127, 154, 165, 170, 204*

Four Hedges, Clare Leighton, 1935 *240, 241L, R, 254*

A Skeleton at the Plough, George Mitchell, 1874 *88*

The Virginians, William Makepeace Thackeray, 1899 *176-177*

TROJAN SPOTTED IN SOUTH SOMERSET

Aeneas and Dido discovered hiding in Low Ham Bath house

Coming full circle, and even older than the story of King Arthur, is the story of Aeneas and Dido which is set in the politically fraught times after the fall of Troy. It is a famous story, which has been relayed to us by Virgil in his Aeneid, which was written down in the late Ist century (29-19BC). What is truly extraordinary is that this story should resurface in the bath house of a large Roman Villa in Low Ham near Langport. The mosaic was discovered in 1938 when a local farmer dug a pit on his farm to bury a dead sheep. The mosaic was excavated after the war in 1946.

The mosaic tells part of the Aeneid in pictures using tessera, instead of lead type. After the Fall of Troy, Aeneas, the wandering Trojan, having been blown there by a storm, pitches up in Carthage on the North African coast. Here he is welcomed, and Venus, his mother, with Cupid's subtle art, plays a trick on Dido, Queen of Carthage, who falls in love with Aeneas. They eventually make love on a hunting trip whilst sheltering from a storm. Afterwards, Dido realises that Aeneas has to fulfil his own prophesy: he nips off to Italy and founds Rome, which scuppers their love affair for good. Distraught, Dido commits suicide by falling on Aeneas's sword. All this is told in five ornate panels.

The Low Ham mosaic is therefore a fitting end to

Aeneas, Cupid, Venus and Dido – Off to the Farmers' Market

Literary Somerset and the last piece of the jigsaw. It takes us right back to the ancient myths and legends which have fuelled our own literature and story telling for two thousand years or more.

To see: The Low Ham mosaic which will be back on display at the County Museum Taunton when it re-opens in Spring 2011. Also see *Roman Mosaics in Somerset* by Bob Croft, Somerset County Archaeologist.

Thirsty Trojans in search of Somerset cider